Published by Ledgewood Press

Author's website
www.deniskingmusic.com

ISBN-13 978-150857-801-7

Also available as a Kindle ebook
ISBN-13 978-1-84396-349-3

And as an audio book from
Amazon, iTunes, and other online retailers.

A CIP catalogue record for this
book is available from the British Library.

Pre-press production
www.ebookversions.com

Acknowledgements

I gratefully acknowledge the assistance of Mike King, Tony King, Moira Feeney, Bruce Francis of Brudenas Productions, Tim Toffoli Graphic Design, Bill Jackson, Karen and Mike Solloway, and James Peach of Timeshift Studios

About Denis King

"I've known Denis King for many years but in spite of that, I would strongly recommend this book."
Barry Cryer

"Denis King changed my life. I remember seeing the King Brothers on TV and I thought, 'Yes! I could do that!' but I was too tall. So I had the operation and the rest is history."
Bill Oddie

"His skills as racy raconteur and dry-as-a-bone humorist are as legendary as his tinkling fingers and classic compositions."
Maureen Lipman

"The happiest memories of the dearest friend. Summer seasons. Shared a house. Lots of golf. My lovely wife, Anne, says he's the best accompanist she's ever sung with."
Ronnie Corbett

"*Standing On The Corner* – yes, one of the great records of that year. Or that month, certainly. I remember the King Brothers as some of the liveliest, freshest, most exciting, oddly-attractive young men I'd ever seen on TV. I know Elvis borrowed a lot of tricks from the King Brothers." **Michael Palin**

"Denis is a trusty friend, a favourite collaborator, a fine musician, and a true original. Though what exactly he was originally, I really couldn't say."
Alan Ayckbourn

"I was star-struck in the 1950s, met DK in the 1960s. Raconteur! Writer! Wit! Actor! Wild swimmer! And joanna-player to die for. Crap cook. Dear old Pal."
Pauline Collins

"DK knows every tune, never misses a note. King's gold!"
John Alderton

To Alexander

KEY CHANGES

A Musical Memoir

Denis King

Edited by Astrid Ronning

Ledgewood Press

Contents

FOREWORD

I'd like us to begin with a brief look at Denis Andrew King, that's Denis with one "n", for "nice", and an Englishman worth crossing an ocean for. Denis is also kind, polite, considerate, dependable, witty, fun, amusing, attractive, talented and, how can I put this, short. I mention this only because he does. Five foot five and three quarters, he says, and was nicknamed Short-Arse at school, but says he doesn't have a complex about it (much, these three quarters seem *pretty important*) and he treats his "diminutive stature", as he calls it, the way he treats most things, with good humor. As a point of reference, Denis comes up to John Cleese's armpit. They actually measured it when they worked together once.

Anyhow, I don't find Denis short. I find him, if you can stand this, perfect kissing height. It's much easier to lean straight over than crane your neck up and back like you're being garrotted. Anyhow I tell him this. And he says he doesn't mind me being taller, he just wishes sometimes he had a few more inches where it counts. Meaning I can't do things like keep the tin foil on the top shelf out of his reach. Unless, of course, I feel like it.

Denis, when he's not trying to reach stuff, is a composer. As a child, then young man, he starred and toured with his

1

brothers in Twice Nightly Variety theatre, playing the London Palladium and the Windmill and countless Empires, Palaces and Hippodromes around the country, he's performed on radio and television, written over 200 themes for TV series, countless jingles for the world of advertising, played the piano here there and everywhere and worked with the best of the best, but his passion is songwriting, specifically for the theatre, and it is to this that he devotes himself when he is not playing golf, or watching it on TV, or telling me about Rory McIlroy's back swing. Fortunately, there is a great deal of money to be made, writing for the theatre. Where, we are not sure, exactly, but I'll let you know if things suddenly pick up.

Denis' other hobbies include ironing, polishing, tidying, coffee mug stain-removing, and trying to get the spot out of the hall carpet where a container of Fairy Liquid emptied three years ago. He also makes beds, dries dishes and puts them away, and does garbage, newspapers, toilets, sinks, tubs and windows, which is where we get into the real teamwork: he hangs onto the ledge and washes, and I point out where he's missed, later. (The nice thing about washing windows in England, of course, is you know how normally as soon as you put the Windolene away it starts bucketing down? Well here it's bucketing down to start with, so no sweat.)

When I first came to England, Denis was temporarily ensconced in a small, unattractive second floor sublet on Belsize Crescent that his soon-to-be ex-wife had found him, having kicked him out of and decided to keep the nice house in Keats Grove for herself, but don't get me started. Every morning Denis would shut himself into a broom closet they call a second bedroom here, into which a piano had been inserted, and compose (or decompose, he says), frantically trying to finish the background music ("scoring" it's called)

Denis on location in Aldershot filming Privates On Parade *in 1982. John Cleese – incidentally leaning down – proves he has the edge on Denis when it comes to who is taller.*

for a television series called *Dick Turpin*, about a highwayman in the 1700s, and there was a lot of music to gallop-by and swordfight-with around the place. I'd find myself moving fast, opening and closing cabinets, chewing, to the beat. Or at least to what I think is the beat; when I was 16 I was Worst Lead Singer in a local rock band and the guys gave me a tambourine once, but took it away about two seconds later because I couldn't count, which was too bad, because I liked how I looked playing it, even though I got big bruises on my thighs.

Denis apologized for being so busy and for all the thundering hooves, but said that ever since he'd done a TV series called *The Adventures of Black Beauty* and the theme had won all kinds of awards, he'd been inundated with

3

horse-type work, but work is work, he said, and you don't complain until it stops. (At which point, I notice, you whinge about it until the cows come home but we're not there yet.)

Speaking of not complaining, I also notice that composers play the same couple of bars over and over and over until you want to yell "Okay! Okay! Make up your mind! Do you want it or don't you??" but what's happening, Den says, is you're not just writing for the piano, you're doing it for the full orchestra (called the "line-up"), meaning the composer hears that same couple of bars not as some mind-numbing license to kill, but as trombones, violas, drums, flugel horns and so on.

"Darling heart," he said one day as I sat at the window watching Belsize Crescent doing its Thames tributary imitation and wondering if the rain might feel like stopping anytime this century, "could you possibly give me a hand sorting out the band parts for tomorrow's session? I'd be extremely grateful."

"Sure!" I said, flattered. "What are band parts?"

Well. Band parts. You have to hear this. When musicians arrive for a recording session, be it for cast albums, television, film, whatever, they don't get handed the whole score, they only get to see his or her own parts i.e. the flute player only gets music marked "FLUTE", the drums player "DRUMS", and so on, and won't know what the alto saxophonists or flugelhorners will be doing, but apparently this doesn't matter, but wait.

How it works is Den composes the whole score on his piano for whatever instruments he thinks right – these days of course aided by computer programs and our techno-musician son, who gets rung about every 20 seconds to find out why there's suddenly no sound or where the trumpets went. Denis would then ring his fixer, named George, who fixed, meaning booked, musicians, not drugs, and drop off the whole score, which was on very large music paper, at his copyist's, a man named John, who would copy out all the musicians' parts individually in black ink onto smaller sheets of music paper and then return them, after ringing our doorbell and mumbling "John here" into the intercom. These smaller sheets were what I'd sort.

They had to be separated not only according to player but stacked in the order in which they'd be recorded. For example, "TROMBONE 1M1" stood for the first music cue for the trombone in Episode 1, and you'd go on up to however many cues there were, "TROMBONE 1M2", "TROMBONE 1M3" and so on, and they'd go face down, starting with 1, and you'd do it for every instrument.

This was all pretty kindergarten stuff and I'd get on the floor of the living room in Belsize Crescent and separate and sort and stack and then check it all a few times to be sure some second violin hadn't sneaked into my first violins making me look bad, and I was very happy to be of musical use.

Next morning at the studio, I'd watch as Den leapt around setting these (excellently sorted) band parts onto the right music stands, who-sits-where having already been figured out by the studio engineer, who also arranged low soundproof walls on wheels to separate the players so their mikes wouldn't pick up spill from other instruments (or something). The musicians would then start filtering in to set up and tune up and swig tea and laugh and joke, and I'd watch and wonder about musician jokes that end with apparent side-splitters like "So he played it in F!", or about whatever made the percussionist decide to become a percussionist, you ought to see the ton of equipment he has to schlep around. (I wanted to play the harp until I realized you had to carry it. I don't much care for skiing either.)

These were all top session players, the cream of Britain's musicians and Denis was always thrilled to have them. They seemed happy to be there too, and were always coming up to me to say how much they liked Den's music and looked forward to his sessions, whereupon I'd beam and say thank you like I taught him everything he knows.

Sharp on the hour, because producers worry about overtime, Denis would be in Toscanini position on the podium, facing the band, conductor's baton in hand, looking cute wearing earphones (called "cans"), and I'd be in the control room watching through a big window and waving and wondering how long before I knocked my Styrofoam coffee cup all over the sound engineer's control desk, and when the engineer signalled "Ready!", Denis would snap his fingers to the right tempo, wait for the film footage to come up on a big screen, say "All right chaps, ladies, a one two three and…" and at exactly the right second, these musicians would play what Denis had written, note perfect, the first time round.

Are you not stunned?

I play the piano a little and am speechless. I'd still be trying to work out what key signature three flats is. It was only a rehearsal, but I'd be knocked out by the talent in the room. Sometimes, after a take, Denis would turn and smile at me through the big window and say, into the mike, "Okay for you, honeybunch?" and I'd give the thumbs up and say "Good for me!" over the Tannoy so everyone could hear, and they'd smile and I'd feel warm and a part of things. It was the closest I'll ever get to being one of the gang. Okay, now here's the real kicker.

We know these musicians don't have the whole score in front of them, right? And are only seeing what their flute or whatever is supposed to be doing? Well, listen to what they have to do: count.

6

Count!

Count the beats to know where to come in, where to stop, where to come in again, where to shut up and so on *all the way through*. Count! I was, and am, hugely, unbelievably, fantastically impressed. And will be out buying a tambourine any day now. Denis says he's always impressed, too, that the fun part for the composer is hearing all those dots of his on paper come alive, and for real, not just on some machine. Whoof! he says. The sound of music! A total high. He says he's always surprised when it sounds okay. What an endearingly modest little thing for the little thing to admit.

And so here I am, still, after 33 years in England, by his side, looking down on him and loving it. Sometimes I miss the States, not so much now but when I first came over, there'd be moments. I didn't want Denis seeing me being homesick, it didn't seem polite, so whenever it hit, I'd splash down the road half a mile to Primrose Hill and make for a bench way up at the top, spread out a plastic carrier bag, and sit. I'd look south through the grey out over the London Zoo to the British Telecom Tower beyond, and go through a few pounds of Kleenex thinking about best friends and parents and maybe those hip waders I left behind in Connecticut. Then I'd leave Primrose Hill, cleansed (wet but cleansed), and walk back to the flat.

And there would be Denis opening the door wearing the colander on his head, which would make me laugh, and the more I laughed, the safer I felt. I may have given up a country, but look at what I got in return. It's one of those sturdy two-handled jobs, too, that fits right over the sink. This is getting so romantic.

Denis is a real find, no question, and not a day goes by that I don't pause for a moment in whatever I'm doing and think how lucky I am and that I was smart enough to grab

Denis volunteering his services on the Sunday morning beach clean-up, Suffolk, 2013. He dressed himself that day, which may be self-evident.

him. He's been doing all the vacuuming, too, since Dolores the cleaning lady went back to the Phillipines. And let us not forget the music, the music! The music that fills, completes, indeed underscores our entire life, our home and, in London, when we lived there, even our street. As soon as you'd get out of your car, you'd hear it. Denis, at the piano. And you'd pause. Strangers walking past would look up at our windows, and smile. For one brief surreal moment you'd see the street as a giant stage set, and the passersby as the chorus of a big Broadway musical, "street extras", all pretending to be separate and unrelated but secretly waiting for their intro, at any second about to launch into some big rip-roaring street scene production number with singing and dancing and cartwheels – and you'd want to shout out proudly: "He's mine!"

But don't worry, the feeling would soon pass. About the same time all the windows slammed shut across the street.

Astrid Ronning
Suffolk, May 2015

OVERTURE

I was sitting at the piano staring at video footage of dancing dustbins for a McDonald's commercial, and trying to be inspired musically but not succeeding, when the phone rang. I grabbed it, delighted for the interruption.

"Denis, it's Michael."

There was no mistaking the clipped, no-nonsense, all-business tones of Michael Codron, theatre producer, with whom I'd recently signed a contract to appear with Maureen Lipman in her new one-woman – and one short piano player – show about the life of the legendary Joyce Grenfell. *Re: Joyce!*, as it was called, was due to begin an eight-week run at London's Fortune Theatre in September. The year was 1988.

I also knew why he was calling. It was about a jacket. A rather important jacket, as it would turn out.

At a production meeting some days earlier, director Alan Strachan and I had discussed what I should wear on stage. I was happy to provide my own dress suit, but Alan wanted me in something different for the first act – the same trousers but another jacket. I said fine, I would contact my tailor in Fulham and have one made. Alan said perfect, he would inform Michael Codron.

Obviously he had done that.

"Michael!" I said, flipping the off switch on the dancing dustbins. "How are you?"

"About this jacket," Michael said. "I'll send you to Bermans and you can find something to fit."

Bermans was a theatrical costumiers.

"Oh," I said. "I'm afraid I can't do that, Michael."

"Why not?"

I explained that I would be appearing in a West End show, I'd be on stage the entire time, and if I'm sitting at the piano for two hours I wanted to be comfortable. On top of which, being short, I'm not easy to fit. I told him I'd have something made by a tailor I knew in Fulham.

There followed a long pause. Michael makes Pinter seem like a chatterbox.

"And how much does your little tailor in Fulham charge for a jacket?" he eventually said, in a cutting tone.

"I think about £400?"

Another silence followed. I waited, as usual. "Michael? Is that all right?"

After another couple of minutes I realised he'd hung up on me.

I immediately phoned Alan Strachan to report that our producer did not appear wildly enthusiastic about paying for me to have a jacket made. Alan said "Nonsense!", he would speak with Michael – that, after all, Maureen had had a whole wardrobe of costumes made, it was only fair, why, I was on stage as much as she was!

"Absolutely!" I couldn't have agreed more and, with slightly more enthusiasm, went back to work on the dancing dustbins.

Alan rang back. Stunned. Michael was completely intransigent, he said, on no account would he pay for a jacket to be made!

I switched off the dustbins again. I told Alan to please tell Mr. Codron that on no account would I be prepared to wear some second-hand thing that didn't fit properly. It's nerve-wracking enough having to be out on stage anyway, you don't want the added worry of everyone thinking you borrowed your big brother's clothes. You want to look decent.

I sensed the jacket becoming a deal-breaker. I also sensed that as I was between agents, I'd have to negotiate the terms of the contract myself, not something I enjoy or am much good at. A week passed. Not a word from Michael Codron. Alan and Maureen were becoming increasingly concerned as rehearsals were looming and they had no piano player.

Having by this time successfully completed a score for the dancing dustbins, I was now immersed in creating something equally musically memorable for a lavatory cleaner, when the phone rang.

"Denis, it's Michael. I've been thinking. You go and get your jacket made from your little tailor in Fulham, pay for it yourself, and I will *hire* it from you for the run of the show, at £20 per week."

"*Hire* it from me," I said. "Are you serious?"

"Yes, I am."

Well, it sounded like a ludicrous proposition but I agreed to it, as we were too far down the road to argue. I signed the contract and proceeded to have a beautiful jacket made by Mr. Dimi Major, my little tailor in Fulham, for £400.

On the 14th of September, 1988, *Re: Joyce!* opened at the Fortune Theatre in London's West End. It was an immediate "hit", a hot ticket, a n d we played to sell-out houses so Michael Codron extended the run of the show

The bespoke dinner jacket that made its stage debut at the Fortune Theatre in September 1988 in Re: Joyce! *– Maureen Lipman's one-woman (and one short piano player) show about the legendary Joyce Grenfell. It was rented from me by producer Michael Codron at £20 per week.*

by a further six weeks, during which period I acquired a new agent, Patricia Macnaughton.

In September of the following year, *Re: Joyce!*, due to overwhelming demand, and following two weeks at Brighton's Theatre Royal to refresh our memories (mine in particular), returned to the West End, this time to the Vaudeville Theatre. I received not only an increase in salary, but my new agent had skilfully negotiated a £5 increase on the weekly hire of my jacket.

We played 1 0 weeks at the Vaudeville, again to

packed houses.

In February of 1990, *Re: Joyce!* had its American premiere at the Long Wharf Theatre in New Haven, Connecticut. My jacket again got a raise (even though I didn't).

Upon returning to England, my deal was renegotiated yet again, this time for a UK tour, and again the jacket did incredibly well out of it. It also got a fee for appearing on my back when *Re: Joyce!* was filmed for BBC Television.

Today, by my reckoning, that £400 jacket has cost Michael Codron in excess of £2,000. And he doesn't even own it, I do. But for some inexplicable reason, he seems to think he got the best of the bargain, and never fails to remind me of this, rather smugly even, on the odd social occasion that we meet.

"How's the jacket doing, Denis?"

"Wonderfully, Michael, thank you. It sends its regards."

Doing *Re: Joyce!* holds countless memories for me. Working with Maureen Lipman, who was breathtaking as Joyce Grenfell. Playing to packed houses. Meeting royalty. Watching Reggie Grenfell's face light up at "seeing his Joyce again". Even watching a friend's husband nod off throughout the show and afterwards tell Maureen what a riveting evening he'd had (one can see a surprising amount from a piano on stage). And so should Michael Codron ever bring *Re: Joyce!* out of cold storage, the jacket and I, though both slightly moth-eaten by now, will be waiting in the wings, at the ready.

But by far the greatest eye-opener of the entire experience was finding myself back on stage again after so many years. I thought I'd given all that up for good.

Which leads me, of course, to The King Brothers.

What is a King Brother? You may well ask.

A King Brother is a former member of a popular British musical trio of yesteryear, once adored by a certain age group, remembered today by few, and when last seen, still alive.

At least I was at breakfast.

Chapter 1

He's Six! He Sings! He Syncopates!

Lying snuggled in the cupboard under the stairs listening to my dad banging out *Deep In The Heart Of Texas* on the old piano in the front room and the sound of grown-ups singing and laughing. My first musical memory. World War II raged overhead, but I felt warm and safe (and have been looking for that cupboard ever since).

Hornchurch, Essex, where my parents had settled after leaving Manchester, had an aerodrome, one of the Battle of Britain air bases, and was a frequent target for German bombers. Before the cupboard under the stairs became our bedroom, whenever the air-raid sirens sounded, my two brothers and I would be awakened up in our room and rushed down to the bottom of the garden – me in my mother's arms – into the Anderson Shelter, where all three boys would be tucked into the top bunk.

An Anderson Shelter, for those who've never heard of one, was issued free by the Government to those earning less than £250 a year, which included my parents, and consisted of 14 sheets of corrugated iron which you fastened together to form a shell 1.8m high, 1.4m wide and 2m long (I had to look this up), which you then half-buried in the ground, covered with soil, and planted with flowers or vegetables. An American journalist over here at the time wrote: "There was a greater danger of being hit by a vegetable marrow falling off the roof of an air-raid shelter than of being struck by a bomb!" In our case, there was more danger of being hit by a King Brother. My brother Tony, I'm told, had a tendency to roll off the top bunk and land on my sleeping father below. Dad, thinking a bomb had struck, would leap up yelling: "Jesus, Mary and Joseph, I'm dead!" – to which Mum would reply: "Don't be so daft, Bill, it's just one of the boys!" and with a weary sigh, turn over.

I was too young to remember, but was assured by my mother, Winifred, years later, that the shelter was cold, damp, usually flooded, prone to a rat or two that needed dispensing with the back of a shovel, and was a thoroughly unpleasant place to spend even a few minutes, let alone the night. The logistics of transporting three little boys down there in the dark, two, maybe three times a night eventually became too much for her: she decided instead to stow us in the cupboard under the stairs and, being a good Catholic, put her trust in God rather than Mr. Anderson. It worked, but the stress of never knowing if your home was going to be there in the morning, or whether you'd even be alive in the morning eventually took its toll on my mother. She became frightened of leaving the house, even to do the shopping, and towards the end of the war had the first of two nervous breakdowns. Dad, I'm fairly certain, wasn't as sympathetic as he might have been.

Bill King wasn't a man much given to sentiment anyway unless he'd had a few drinks in him, whereupon his Irish roots would surface, his eyes would fill and he'd be serenading whoever was left in the pub with *I'll Take You Home Again, Kathleen*. He worked as a planning engineer at the Ford Motor Company in Dagenham, East London and because during the war Ford was involved in making armaments, Dad, being in what was called a "reserved occupation", was exempt from military service. He "did his bit" however, by joining the Auxiliary Fire Service, but I don't think he enjoyed it or was even particularly good at it since he was known to faint at the sight of blood. He had an axe and a bell, though (which I still have), and that impressed me. He'd often be called out at night to assist in digging out incendiary bombs from blazing houses, coming home exhausted and covered in soot. My mum told me that on one such occasion he popped his head into the cupboard under the stairs, looking for something, forgetting we were there, and I didn't recognise him and screamed bloody murder (as did he). After Dad died, in 1982, we discovered six, small, hand-scrawled notebooks in which he'd kept meticulous records of the daily air-raid sirens and the all-clears, noting when they'd sounded, when they'd stopped, what damage had occurred where; five whole years of notes consisting entirely of numbers, dates and weather reports, nothing personal at all, apart from these two entries:

"Baby stillborn," he wrote on the 14th of March, 1943. "Terribly disappointed but Win taking it like a brick. It was a girl." And then on the 9th of May, 1945 (the day after VE Day): "Felt bad all day, no drink to be had in Hornchurch district."

Sad to say, if I had to guess which event was the more traumatic for him, my money might be on the lack of local booze. Dad must have been absolutely thrilled when

William and Winifred King, devoted parents of Michael, Tony, Denis, and Moira. On a night out, Manchester, England, circa 1930.

the Americans entered the war in 1942 and, overnight, Hornchurch became full of GIs, many of whom gravitated, along with their Lucky Strikes and bottles of bourbon, towards Dad's local pub, The Bull, whose principal offering at the time was only warm beer. Always up for a party, Bill, after closing time, would invite these GIs back to the house for a noisy sing-song around the piano – and that's what I heard, lying snuggled and safe inside the cupboard under the stairs.

Fortunately, my mother Win enjoyed a knees-up as much as my dad – she had a sweet, bell-like voice I could hear above all the others, however raucous the party – and on any given night there would be at least a dozen GIs present, plus Irish drinking mates, neighbours, friends, all crammed into our front room. One of the Yanks would invariably stick his head into our cupboard and say "Hey kids, want some candy?" and we'd be showered with Hershey Bars and Wrigleys Juicy Fruit chewing gum, all of which we'd immediately stuff into our mouths and fall asleep savouring, events which I am now convinced should come under the heading "War Crimes", you should see what I've had to shell out over the years on bridges and crowns. I think in some respects Dad was almost sorry to see the war end.

But he soon had another focus, one that was to last him a good 25 years, and it was all down to the fact that he happened to possess an extraordinary musical ear.

As well as being able to drink practically anything, and repair practically anything, from a broken lamp to a toilet to a fan-belt or a manifold, whatever that is – my idea of car repair is dropping it off at Scarlett's Garage over in Westleton – Dad could also play a tune on practically anything. Violin, harmonica, accordion, guitar, banjo, saxophone, piano, comb and paper, any instrument put in front of him he could make a sound on – and a pretty good one – and without having had any music lessons on any of them. And as soon as he noticed that I had inherited this musical ear of his, I became his sole focus. Not counting the pub.

As the family story goes, apparently I sat down at the piano in the front room one day, aged five, and played precisely what my father had just played, *Don't Fence Me In*. Dad's jaw dropped and his pipe fell out of his mouth.

"Win! Win!" he cried. "Look at this!" and when my mother came in from the kitchen, Dad told me to play it again, which I did, and then her jaw dropped open.

I don't remember any of it. And can't tell you how I was able to do what I did, because I don't know. My hands, as they still do today, just sort of... knew where to go. Dad immediately found me a piano teacher, a bastard called Alec College.

Mr. College, who I most definitely do remember, would insist I keep my hands in a fixed position as I played, wrists raised as if gripping an invisible railing, and if ever they slipped back to a more comfortable position, for example, one in which I could actually play – which they did, frequently – he would strike me sharply on the knuckles with a black and brown striped wooden ruler. I think it's safe to say I learned nothing from Mr. College except possibly a dislike of rulers and Mr. College himself.

Dad insisted I practise an hour a day and I'd be locked in the front room to ensure this happened. I soon discovered I had a knack for being able to play the same piece over and over from memory while at the same time reading a comic book. This skill is unfortunately not one that has been especially useful in later life, although it does enable me to "underscore" myself here and there if needs be, meaning I can tinkle a little background music while simultaneously telling a story to an audience. My wife equates this talent with whisking hollandaise while speaking on the phone to one's mother in America while watching *University Challenge* and yelling out the correct answer.

My father soon decided I should perform, and arranged for me to appear at the Towers Cinema, Hornchurch. Saturday morning film shows for children were commonplace in 1946 and often included a live act. Next to my name on the programme was the slogan "He's Six! He Sings! He Syncopates!" (which sounds to me like a Bill King original). I remember it. Trotting fearlessly out onto the stage, holding my little banjolele – a four-stringed instrument like a mini banjo – then playing and singing a jolly rendition of *Bell Bottom Trousers* which, for some reason, I did in a Cockney accent.

BELL BOTTOM TROUSERS,
COAT OF NAVY BLUE,
SHE LOVES A SAILOR
AND HE LOVES HER TOO,
WHEN THEY'RE TOGETHER
HE THRILLS HER THROUGH AND THROUGH
WITH HIS BELL BOTTOM TROUSERS,
COAT OF NAVY BLUE...

Rapturous applause followed, possibly in eager anticipation of *Flash Gordon*, the Saturday morning serial that came next, but I can still see Grandpa King watching from the back of the cinema. Afterwards, I ran up the aisle into his arms, he lifted me up and with tears in his eyes pressed half a crown into my tiny hand. My first paid job. It would be nice to think I still have it, framed, but I imagine it went to help pay the milk bill. Dad, spurred on by my Towers Cinema success, immediately began entering me in local talent competitions. Press coverage from this period is slim but according to a 1949 issue of the *Ford Motor Company News*, which I happen to have in my possession, I auditioned for the Carroll Levis Show at the Camberwell Theatre and was ruled too young to appear, but "allowed to entertain in an

Displaying my early accordion technique; an instrument I don't recall ever playing since.

unofficial capacity", whatever that means. My father then decided to expand the act.

My eldest brother, Mike, despite a limited musical ability, needed no encouragement. Dad taught him a few chords on the guitar, while I played the piano and accordion and sang harmony. Neither of our voices had broken and our repertoire was limited to three songs: *Far Away Places*, *When The Saints Go Marching In* and *Hear My Song, Violetta*. Nevertheless, and I speak with some authority here, thanks to Mrs. Winifred King's foresight in keeping scrapbooks of her sons' triumphs, it seems we consistently brought the house down at such veritable venues as the Railway Hotel, Dagenham (in aid of The Ford Angling Society), the Rex Cinema Collier Row (where we won a silver cup) and I wouldn't be at all surprised if the audience at the Ford Canine Section's First Smoking Concert 1951 is still talking about us.

Mike and I made a few recordings – Dad's idea – in one of those little booths they had at the time where you'd go in and pay two shillings (about 10p), pull the curtain, and come out with a 78rpm acetate disc of yourselves singing, which you'd then rush home to play on your wind-up gramophone – recordings which will unfortunately never get the chance to be traded for vast sums on eBay since they no longer exist, since Mike's ex in-laws, scrap metal merchants in Shepherd's Bush, lost them, or perhaps made coasters out of them.

Inevitably, it dawned on my father that a duo could very easily become a trio, at which point Tony, my middle brother, was press-ganged into the act. A man named Cyril, from the Ford Motor Company, an establishment which seems to be featuring more and more in our career, played the double bass in a local string quartet and Dad persuaded him to give Tony lessons. Tony, by his own admission, was not naturally musically gifted, but through sheer determination and perseverance and practice he became a more than competent bass player. In fact, all these years later, he's only recently given it up: he'd been enjoying playing in a local pit orchestra down in Kent until he began suffering from a form of narcolepsy – when the drummer started having to prod him awake for each number with his drumstick Tony decided it might be time to put the bass in moth balls and go and nod off in front of the TV instead.

Thus were The King Brothers born, whether we liked it or not. Three young, naïve Essex boys, about to be

25

The newly formed King Brothers, Hornchurch, 1951. The KBs on our matching shirts having been lovingly embroidered by our mum, Win.

thrown into the starry, seductive and often seedy world of showbiz. For William and Winifred King of 12, Grey Towers Avenue, Hornchurch, planning engineer at the

Ford Motor Company, and housewife – life was to become decidedly different. For us, the brothers, life was just going to be – well, life.

Chapter 2

WE WANNA SAY HELLO,
WE WANNA SEE YOU SMILE!

"Mum Wrote Their Signature Tune!" was the eye-catching headline in the October 1952 *Briggs Motor Bodies News*, a division of the Ford Motor Company. I like to imagine an army of panel-beaters downing tools and racing off to get their copy.

The previous year, my mother had written to the BBC to try and get an audition for Mike and me but was told I was too young. After Tony joined the act she wrote again and this time we were accepted. Without wishing to give the impression I spend my days scouring the world's press for inaccuracies in King Brothers reportage, I am obliged to mention here that contrary to every biog or blurb I've ever read on the subject, we did *not* appear on Huw Weldon's TV show *All Your Own*, I never even met the man. Our first appearance on television was in 1952 on *Shop Window*.

This was a live broadcast transmitted from Studio G,

Lime Grove, Shepherd's Bush. The purpose of the show was to introduce unknown actors and performers and give them the opportunity of working on camera with established stars. On the first show in which we appeared, Constance Cummings and Leslie Henson were the established actors and the unknowns were Dilys Laye and Ronald Lewis. A man named Henry Caldwell produced the show and introduced each act from his revolving chair in the control room with a camera pointed at him, a revolutionary technique at the time.

Mum and Dad bought their first television, a 12in bulky cabinet model made by Kolster-Brandes, especially to watch our debut. The initials KB on the side of the box happened to match those of the King Brothers, something that tickled Dad from the moment it arrived and he enjoyed pointing out this extraordinary coincidence to anyone who came to marvel at the new acquisition. *Shop Window* went out on a Monday night at 8pm. When our turn came and Henry Caldwell introduced us – me perched on a telephone directory because the piano stool wasn't high enough (story of my life) – we launched into our rousing opening number, Winifred King's version of *I Wanna Say Hello!*, a popular song at the time. This we followed with *Shine On Harvest Moon* and the act ended with me doing an impersonation of Rose " The Chee-Chee Girl" Murphy, singing her hit *Me And My Shadow*, which strikes me now as a curious choice since Rose Murphy was a large black American singer/piano player, and I wasn't, and am still not, but the number went over surprisingly well.

"In 10 years' time," wrote TV critic Peter Black in *The Daily Mail* the following morning, "we may expect to see these boys supporting the American top of the bill at the Palladium and the youngest, Dennis, is a genuine

Headlining in The Ford News, *Bill King's favourite reading matter. Although I look about nine I was, in fact, 13 in this photo.*

infant phenomenon. At 13 he not only plays and sings with forbidding nonchalance, he smiles as relentlessly as a politician fighting a by-election."

An excellent notice, although Peter Black was wrong on two counts. The King Brothers got to the Palladium supporting American star Howard Keel within four years, not 10, and, infinitely more important, there's only one "N" in Denis. Far more exciting to my father, I imagine, was the headline in that week's *Ford News*: "SONS OF FORD MAN ON TV SHOW!"

He and my mother became local celebrities overnight.

In those days, anyone who owned a television set (there were 1.4 million TVs in the UK in 1952) would have seen the show because there was only one channel. My parents couldn't leave the house without being congratulated on having such "famous" sons. Dad acquired new status at work.

"Saw your boys on the telly last night, Bill! Bloody marvellous!"

He loved the sudden attention and lapped up the praise in the machine shop. A pint and a pipe and tinkering under a Ford car might have their moments, but for Dad, nothing beat boasting about his lads to anyone who would listen. My sister Moira was not quite five when we first appeared on television. When speaking to her about these memoirs, she told me something that neither my brothers nor I had been aware of. It seems from the moment of her birth, Moira had been Dad's little princess. He doted on her, the shining apple of his eye, and every afternoon when he returned from work she'd be waiting excitedly at the front gate then rush to greet him, shrieking with delight as he'd swoop her up into his arms. Then came a day, which I regret to say coincides exactly with The King Brothers' overnight success, when Moira rushed to the gate to meet Dad, arms outstretched, and he walked straight past her and into the house. She told me that from that moment on he never paid much attention to her and that for many years she never thought he even liked her very much.

I'd had no idea how our success had affected her. None. I just think of her as always laughing and happy and being excited at meeting the famous people we'd bring home, people you normally wouldn't run into in Buckhurst Hill. Sean Connery, for instance. He arrived in a kilt one New Year's Eve and Tony recalls teasing Moira relentlessly, accusing her of crawling on the floor trying to see what was under the kilt, until she ran off in tears.

Bill King, Daughter Ignorer, decided his three boys would benefit from some professional musical tuition, so my brothers and I began traveling into London once a week to the Central School of Dance Music where Mike had guitar lessons from Ivor Mairants, who ran the school, Tony was taught bass by Joe Muddell, a well-known bass player, and my piano teacher was Dennis Wilson, a lovely man who later went on to write the theme for *Fawlty Towers*. Dad also secured for us a manager – of sorts – in Mr. Ron Sensier, somebody he knew from the Ford Motor Company, and it was Ron's job to find us work and advise us on material.

Ron Sensier was hardly Ford's answer to Swifty Lazar, Hollywood agent extraordinaire, given that Ron normally installed head gaskets and wasn't remotely connected to show business, so how we actually got any gigs remains a mystery, but we seemed to be busy, mostly at weekends, because at 13, I was still at school. Tony had left at 15, Mike was then 17 and working part-time for a butcher. As young King Brothers we toured US Air Force bases around the country, Dad driving us in the trusty Ford (and sweet-talking his way into every PX for cheap cigarettes), we made another

Shop Window TV appearance and performed at numerous local charity concerts. At the Hornchurch and Upminster Theatre Club, for instance, I see here that we not only helped raise funds for their Junior Group, we also "brought welcome relief to an otherwise heavy evening". And, at the Gaumont State Cinema, Kilburn, we – wholly unintentionally – brought comic relief.

With over 4,000 seats, the Gaumont State was the biggest cinema in the country. The design was inspired by the Empire State Building in New York. Its fully-equipped stage was one of the largest ever built, being 100ft wide and 50ft deep, and the orchestra pit was on a hydraulic lift that could be raised to stage level. The producer of the concert had the novel idea of setting The King Brothers on this lift, pre-set in the bowels of the theatre, and as our number began, we would be slowly raised up to normal stage level to perform our act, after which we'd be lowered back down. It worked perfectly in rehearsal.

On the night, we were introduced and, down below, on cue, we launched into our song as the lift began its ascent.

    RUNNING WILD, OUT OF CONTROL
    RUNNING WILD, MIGHTY BOLD
    FEELING GAY, RECKLESS TOO
    JUST A SMILE, ALL THE WHILE, NEVER BLUE...

At which point the lift shuddered and stopped. The top halves of Mike and Tony were in view but as I was sitting at the piano when things ground to a halt, my head level with the pit rail, all the audience could see of me was from the nose upwards, like one of those cartoon characters one draws, looking over a fence. Not knowing

34

what else to do, we carried on playing and singing as if nothing were wrong.

ALWAYS GOING, DON'T KNOW WHERE
ALWAYS SHOWING, I DON'T CARE...

The audience started to titter. Below us, all hell was breaking loose as stagehands shouted and hammered and banged on the mechanism.

AIN'T GOT NOBODY, IT AIN'T WORTHWHILE
ALL ALONE, RUNNING WILD...

Titters grew into chuckles, which grew into guffaws, and by the time we reached my piano solo we were getting more laughs than the comedian who'd preceded us. In the middle of it, there was a sudden lurch and the lift started to move again. Expectations grew, but not for long. The lift went down, not up. The audience became hysterical. My head gradually disappeared from view, Tony's and Mike's followed, and our final chorus was sung underneath the stage to a bunch of bewildered, head-scratching stagehands. The Gaumont State, for your information, is now a Grade II listed building (nothing to do with the Disappearing King Brothers) and has recently been bought by a church.

The Catholic Stage Guild Concert in February of 1953 at the Adelphi Theatre in London and compered by Ted Kavanagh was, by contrast, technically less eventful, but had a much bigger impact on our career. We shared the bill with, in no particular order, Wilfred Pickles, Binnie Hale, Nancy and Babe Bridges (two Australian xylophonists), Moira Lister, Bebe Daniels and Ben Lyon (he discovered Marilyn Monroe), Gilbert Harding (whose hand Mike suddenly felt on his backside while waiting in the wings), Eamonn Andrews, Jack Cruise, Dame Ninette de Valois and Max Bygraves. All good Catholics (more or less).

"These three young Catholic entertainers are a mixture of sophistication and boyish ingenuousness!" cried *The Catholic Times*. Bygraves' wife, Blossom, apparently thought so, too, and suggested to husband Max that we appear on his forthcoming television show, *A Good Idea, Son!* which, shortly thereafter, we did.

The show, in May of 1953, was broadcast and performed live on a Saturday night at 9.30pm. Written by Eric Sykes, it featured, among others, Belita, an American ice-skater, someone named Olgalita Mayne, someone else named Lillemor Knudsen (a blonde with very large breasts), The Windmill Girls, and Jean Marsh (whose breasts I don't remember but she went on to write, with Eileen Atkins, *Upstairs Downstairs*). The show was huge, meaning there was nothing else to watch, and The King Brothers' act received quite a bit of attention and publicity. Chesney Allen of Flanagan and Allen fame was by then a successful agent and, having seen the show, and possibly read our mention in *The Sporting Review*, "These boys are boogie-woogie-ists!", contacted us to ask if we'd be interested in doing some theatre.

And back then, theatre meant only one thing.

Chapter 3

TWICE NIGHTLY

Twice Nightly Variety had its origins in Music Hall and by the mid Fifties was still one of the most popular forms of entertainment. Practically every town in the country had a Variety theatre or two, usually called The Empire or The Palace, and The King Brothers appeared at most of them. The Newcastle Palace, Leicester Palace, Hull Palace, East Ham Palace, Newcastle Empire, Leeds Empire, Liverpool Empire, Glasgow Empire, Finsbury Park Empire – after a while they all started to look the same. You'd be a week here, a week there, perhaps a week off then back on the train to somewhere else. You'd play two shows a night and a matinée on Saturday then move on, sometimes as a whole company, sometimes not. Each act was independent. You might work with, say, Pop White & Stagger ("Half Dancers – Half Crackers!") one week and The Apex Four ("Sensational Equilibrists") the next, or never run into any of them ever again. Looking at old theatre posters I see that The King

Brothers also worked with a Mr. Bill Ken-Dall ("Almost a Conjuror!"), Vivian et Passi ("Continental Comedy Jugglers"), Max River's Six Wynettes ("Setting the Tempo with a Perfect Swing!") and American contortionist Betsy Ross ("She Bends Over Backwards To Please!"), none of whom I remember much about except Betsy liked her gin and also my brother Mike, who I think was a bit scared of her, particularly when she'd walk around backwards with her head between her legs.

But whether you liked them or not, all of the speciality acts, every single one of them, the jugglers, the ventriloquists, the escapologists, illusionists, strong men, strong women, acrobats, animal acts, mime acts, magicians, mind-readers – were professionals, and good at what they did. You might wonder how some of them came up with the idea for their act to begin with, like the man we worked with who hit himself over the head with a tin tray while singing *Ghost Riders In The Sky*, but you had to at least give them credit for being able to make a living at it. My favourite speciality act was Henri Vadden and his wheel.

Monsieur Vadden, who spoke as if he hailed more from Pontefract than from Paris, had a strong man act. Stocky, of medium height, wearing a moth-eaten leopard-skin (that was more moth than leopard) and a pair of Roman sandals that criss-crossed up to his knees, Henri began his act with a predictable strong man routine involving the bending of iron bars, the tearing of telephone directories, the breaking of bricks with his bare fists and so on. But as we discovered the first time we were on the bill with him, there was more to his act than the audience out front would ever know.

As Henri approached his grand finale, the music for which we could hear over the Tannoy, my brothers and

Twice Nightly Variety poster from the Manchester Hippodrome, from the late 1950s.

I became aware of a flurry of activity backstage. Dressing room doors opened, conversations stopped, and there was a stampede down the stairs as fellow performers crowded into the wings and jostled for a good view of the stage. Curious, we hurried after them.

A drum roll began. Henri produced a Kaiser

Wilhelm World War I helmet, the kind with a metal spike on top, and strapped it onto his head. Next to him was an enormous cartwheel, the old wooden kind with an iron rim, and this he lifted up, then heaved, spinning, into the air. Immediately, he adopted a crouch position. Everyone backstage tensed.

When the cartwheel came down, Henri caught it on the spike of his helmet and, upon impact, the force of which would have been enough to flatten a horse, Henri, eyes closed, and, loud enough for us to hear but inaudible to the audience, cried out through gritted teeth, *"Oh, Christ!"*

His expression of agony was instantly replaced by a forced and rather sickly smile as, with a triumphant "Ta-Da!" from the band, Henri stood up and received his applause.

Nothing quite sums up the bittersweet taste of show business, for me, as that image.

I once related this story to my dear friend, the wonderful writer Jack Rosenthal, who started laughing so much just imagining the poor man having to do this night after night for years on end, that he couldn't speak, and from then on I had only to whisper the name "Henri Vadden" in Jack's ear – at the theatre in the middle of a quiet moment or when he had a mouth full of fishballs – and that was it, he'd be off. Monsieur Vadden had no idea, I'm sure, of the unmitigated pleasure his act has brought to so many people or that he would be remembered for so long.

Sad to say, the majority of Variety acts eventually disappeared without a trace. A few, though, went on to bigger and better things. At the Newcastle Palace, The King Brothers shared the bill with two then unknown comedians, Eric Morecambe and Ernie Wise. We headlined at the New Theatre, Cardiff with an up and coming all-round performer named Bruce Forsyth. Val Doonican was a member of the Four Ramblers, an Irish singing group on the bill with us at Middlesbrough. Olivia Newton-John was part of an Australian girl duo we worked with at the Wolverhampton Grand, and at a Working Men's Club in Nelson, Lancashire, we discovered a funny young Liverpool comedian named Jimmy Tarbuck. You just knew you hadn't heard the last of them, that they all had that special something.

In 1954, the "special something" for The King Brothers was something called *Bouncing Ball Boogie*. This was the brainchild of Mr. Ron Sensier, aforementioned head-gasket-fitter at Ford's and less-than-dynamic King Brothers manager, and it was, I don't think I am alone in saying this, a disastrous idea start to finish. The song was made famous by Frankie "Sugar Chile" Robinson, "Chile" as in short for "child", but incorrectly pronounced "chilly", by Mr. Sensier, who insisted that the number would be "a surefire showstopper for The King Brothers". It began like this:

YOU BOUNCE IT DOWN LOW
YOU BOUNCE IT UP HIGH
YOU BOUNCE IT IN THE MIDDLE
OH ME OH MY
IT'S THE BOUNCIN' BALL BOOGIE
THE BOUNCIN' BALL BOOGIE
THE BOUNCIN' BALL BOOGIE
I LOVE TO BOUNCE IT ALL THE TIME...

And so on.

Ron Sensier then brought on board an ageing American choreographer named Quentin Foster (probably no more than 40) and Mr. Foster's inspired contribution to the number was the introduction of a real rubber ball, the idea being that the three of us would sing and play instruments and bounce a ball all at the same time. The ball was red and about the size of a basketball. Mr. Foster had worked out a complicated routine whereby we'd sing a chorus of the song, sans ball, itself hidden from view behind Tony's double bass, and at the start of the second chorus, Tony, still playing and singing, would produce the ball and bounce it to me. I, still playing and singing, would bounce it to Mike, and Mike, still playing and singing, would bounce it back to Tony. The ball-bouncing would continue for the rest of the chorus, at which point Tony, still playing and singing, would return it to its home behind the bass. It's easy to see why the world at large has never heard of Quentin Foster.

Despite limited success at rehearsals, he was convinced it would all be fine.

The King Brothers arrived off the train at West Hartlepool on a Sunday evening with suitcases, Tony's bass, Mike's guitar, and the ball. I was at the mercy of whatever piano the local theatre provided. It was the start of a six-week tour.

Monday morning was the usual 10am band call, which is when the acts on the bill present their music to the musical director and the pit band to run through the numbers. It was important to get there early in case one of the other acts happened to be using the same song as you were; things were on a first come first served basis and whoever lost out would have to find a replacement song for that week. On this occasion, however, we were quite safe. Curiously, no one else was doing *Bouncing Ball Boogie*. We didn't rehearse with the ball for the band call or even mention it to Sid, the musical director, as it was intended to be a big surprise. Which it was.

After our rehearsal, Mike and Tony went off to kill time at the cinema while I, as usual, spent the afternoon sitting at the back of a classroom at the local secondary modern. Being only 14, I was required by law to attend school wherever we were. I can't think that I learned one thing. Often, the local accents were so strong I had no idea what anyone was even saying. Being a Londoner, I was a curiosity myself initially, but after the first hour I was usually ignored by everyone, including the teachers. I suppose it was easier to hand me a book and point to a chair at the back than involve me in anything the class had been doing.

When the school bell rang at 4pm that day in West Hartlepool I rushed back to our "digs", had a quick cheese sandwich and a cup of tea with my brothers, and we got ourselves over to the Empire Theatre for 5.30pm. The first show was at 6.15pm, the second at 8.30pm. We went to our dressing room, applied our stage make-up (Leichner Nos 5 and 9), changed into shirts and ties and our jackets with "KB" on the breast pocket, lovingly sewn on by our mother, Mrs. Winifred King, and made our way to the wings, with the ball, to await our entrance.

When our cue came, we scurried on stage, found our positions which had been marked out earlier, and quickly and quietly set up behind a front cloth while on the other side of it a comedian was finishing his act. As the curtain rose on "Britain's Youngest Rhythm Aces", we were primed and ready with our broad, fixed smiles in place and red rubber ball discreetly hidden behind Tony's bass. Our first two numbers, *Shortnin' Bread* and *A Sky Blue Shirt And A Rainbow Tie* went swimmingly, for a wet Monday night at West Hartlepool with a handful of people in the audience. We were saving

43

Bouncing Ball Boogie for the grand finale.

We began the song and it went as rehearsed, but then came the second chorus: the "ball" chorus. In retrospect, I think the crux of the problem, not counting the whole thing being a terrible idea to begin with, was Tony's initial difficulty in retrieving the ball from behind his bass, because by the time he'd got a good grip on it, the song had moved on one bar. This meant any future ball bouncing would occur on the wrong beat. Not the end of the world, but enough to be disconcerting, especially to someone who wasn't that confident to begin with, which included all of us.

Tony, undeterred, still playing and singing, attempted to bounce the ball over to me. Unfortunately, it deflected off the side of the piano and made a beeline for Mike. Mike, still playing and singing, and wholly unprepared for the sudden change of choreography, somehow managed to strike the ball using the end of his guitar, rather like a cricket bat, and back it shot in my direction.

I, still playing and singing, stuck my hand out to grab the ball but succeeded only in punching it, whereupon it shot straight down into the orchestra pit and hit the musical director on the head. This was the first time Sid had ever seen the ball and he was, not unreasonably, surprised. That surprise soon turned to fury, as not only did the ball bounce off his forehead, it then bounced down to knock all his music for the entire evening off its stand and send it flying throughout the orchestra pit. This didn't affect us, musically at least, since we accompanied ourselves, but acts that followed would need a conductor with music in front of him.

We watched Sid on his hands and knees frantically gathering up pages of scores as, ball-less, we carried on, smiling and singing and playing until the end of our song, after which there was a smattering of applause, most of it, I suspect, based on pity.

As we came forward to take our bow, Sid stood up looking somewhat dishevelled, steaming, clutching a wad of music, and the red ball, which he then hurled at us, with some force, greatly hastening our exit. I ducked, the ball bounced off Tony's bass and into the audience, never to be seen again. Neither Ron Sensier nor Quentin Foster witnessed the first – and last – performance of *Bouncing Ball Boogie*, staying well out of range in London, and we never saw them again, either.

At the interval, abject apologies to Sid were required, as well as a significant change of repertoire for The King Brothers for the second house that evening.

Chapter 4

KINGS OF THE ROAD

I wouldn't entertain for a second letting my son go off touring in show business at the age of 13, chaperoned only by a 17-year-old, nor would the authorities these days even allow it, but my parents obviously thought nothing of letting their three young lads loose around the country for weeks on our own when most boys of our age had to be home every night by 10 at the latest. Maybe they thought there was safety in numbers. Maybe there was. I just know that after every tour I couldn't wait to get home. Even a week seemed such a long time to be away.

Theatrical "digs" — the places you stayed — were not, at least in those days, anywhere you'd want to call "home" or spend any more time than necessary. You usually arranged them by post prior to arriving in a city, and they looked remarkably similar wherever you were: a small terraced house, run by a Mrs. Somebody, occasionally a Miss. Only rarely were you aware of a

Mister, perhaps a man's voice behind a closed door. Usually two or three rooms of the house would be let, often to other artists on the bill that week. The room would cost between £4 and £8 per week for the three of us and would include breakfast and an evening meal after the show. I use the word "meal" in its broadest sense.

My brothers and I would share a room that had either three narrow single beds or a single and a double. Mike, being the eldest, invariably snared the single. Sheets were thin and often damp. There would be linoleum on the floor, a single light bulb hanging from the ceiling, a gas fire with a meter by the side of it that took a shilling (five pence), and the room was always cold. Hot water for a bath was extra. You could have a lie-in in the morning, but only until 8.30am. Any later and you sacrificed breakfast, not always a bad thing. Soggy fried bread, runny tinned tomatoes with a few baked beans swimming around, undercooked bacon, overcooked fried egg, cold toast and a cup of tea. If ever you came across digs where the landlady cared about the food it was such a novelty that you talked about it for weeks afterwards.

Mrs. McKay's in Manchester was known in the digs world as the Ritz of the Northwest. It was clean and warm and dry and had edible, if not memorable food. If you could get in at Mrs. McKay's, you were set for the week, although you had to put up with her class system. She would never admit to it, but a hierarchy existed, with a clear divide being made between actors from the legitimate theatre and those of us from lowly Variety. Her digs consisted of two interconnecting semi-detached houses which had a common lounge and dining room. The actors were housed in one house, the Variety performers in the other, and Mrs. McKay made it very clear as to which group was the more important. The actors got the hottest tea or toast, the freshest sandwiches, and the undivided attention of a fawning Basil Fawlty-ish landlady. I can still hear her fussing over actor Geoffrey Palmer in the dining room.

Publicity shot of the King Brothers circa 1952, preparing for another jaunt around England performing in Twice Nightly Variety. The shirts were dark and light blue, I recall. We wore whatever we could find three of.

"Is everything quite to your satisfaction, Mr. Palmer?" she would enquire in an affected accent. Geoffrey was always hugely embarrassed by the attention, sheepishly glancing over to our side of the room where we humble Variety folk sat lonely and forgotten, hungrily eyeing any crumbs of toast that had fallen on the floor.

When you reported to the stage-door of the theatre in whichever city you were playing, the rule of thumb was to tell the stage-doorkeeper where you'd be staying for the week – usually digs, but if you were feeling flush, a pub. The stage-doorman almost always had a limp and a hearing problem, something that Kenny Earle, part of a comedy double act called Earle & Vaughan with whom we worked a lot, would invariably put to the test. Whenever he was asked: "Wheraya stayin' this week, Mister Earle?", Kenny would mumble: "The C**t and Compass."

There would be a pause, during which the rest of us crowded into the dingy entry waiting our turn tried to keep a straight face.

"Ah beg yer pardon, Mister Earle...?"

Kenny would then reply, clearly and distinctly, "At Mrs. Hunters in Railway Terrace!" and the stage-doorman, after another pause, would nod and note it down.

If you had neglected to arrange accommodation in advance, you'd get a list of local addresses from the stage-doorman and make your own arrangements, a practice which still exists today. While doing a week at the Empire Theatre in Nottingham, we hadn't managed to book anywhere to stay and ended up in desperately grim lodgings, a commercial guest house catering mainly for lorry drivers and run by an enormous woman in a stained floral house dress who sang hymns loudly, beginning at approximately 6.30am.

Our first morning there, Mike and I were awakened by the strains of *Nearer My God To Thee* coming from somewhere downstairs and sat bolt upright in time to see a figure wearing a patterned head scarf bending over Tony's bed, an unsavoury-looking character with a ferret-like face, a permanent drip on the end of his nose, and who was in the process of pulling back Tony's covers.

"Hey!" we yelled. "What are you doing!"

The man jumped, looked around, and shot out of the room. It was later explained that he was a "mentally-retarded window cleaner". We checked out after breakfast. I recall being only mildly disturbed by the experience, nothing more. I doubt we even mentioned it to our parents. We'd certainly never heard the word "paedophile" and no one had even told us to look out for them. Perhaps it was simply a more innocent age, at least on the surface. The first time we were even aware of the *existence* of homosexuality, though we weren't quite sure what it was, was when we shared a dressing room with Freddie Hardy in Southport in 1954.

A lively, kind little man with a terrible wig who wore make-up in the daytime was how we saw him. Freddie referred to himself as "Mother", as in "Come to Mother, Mother will fix it!" and he trotted around making sure everyone was happy and had what they needed. There was nothing predatory about him. You'd think that three young fresh-faced boys might have been an obvious target unchaperoned on the Variety circuit, wouldn't you, but other than Mike feeling Gilbert Harding's hand on his backside in the wings and a well-known (and still very much alive) choreographer once chasing me around his living-room sofa, The King Brothers were left alone. Older artists, which almost all of them were, felt protective towards us. They didn't even swear much around us, in fact, didn't swear much at all. Certainly never on stage. Comedy acts might contain the occasional double entendre but nothing stronger. People would have been shocked. I remember comedian Tommy Cooper at an after-show party at a hotel in Brighton. My parents had come down to see us and we'd invited them along. Cooper was holding court telling jokes.

"Look at this!" he said. "An Eskimo having a pee!", at which point he opened his flies and out fell a fistful of ice cubes. My dad laughed, but my mother was horrified.

At 14, sex wasn't discussed, definitely not by me nor my brothers (nor my parents), and despite sharing bedrooms and dressing rooms, we never even saw one another naked, we'd modestly turn our backs when undressing. Mike had his first romance at the age of 18 (a dancer in a summer season), but that, too, was innocent. Chorus girls were often barely 16, often local and, contrary to what you might think, their morals were generally high. On top of which we were "good Catholic boys". At least we were then. When we stayed at a Mrs. Bradley's digs in Leeds, which comedians Mike and Bernie Winters had recommended, saying we'd have an interesting week because it was a *very friendly place* once you got used to the phone ringing at all hours and high heels clattering on the stairs, it took us a couple of days before we twigged that we were in fact living in a brothel. Not that this changed anything, I think the only physical attention I received there was a fond pat on the head as one of the girls rushed past me up the stairs, but it could have been her elbow.

Had the young, clean-cut King Brothers been discovered living in a brothel it would have made headlines, for sure, but the media was nothing like as intrusive as it is now. The papers had better things to write about. That said, if word did get out, whole careers could be ruined by what was then considered immoral behaviour. In 1955 in Morecambe, when comedian Max Wall left his wife and two children to take up with a beauty queen, the ensuing scandal finished him overnight. He couldn't get work and eventually had to get a job as a gardener on the island of Jersey. It took until the 1980s for him to be accepted back into the profession, where he eventually re-established himself as not only the wonderful comedian he'd been, but a great actor. And had the press got hold of David Whitfield's quite repellent way of signing his autograph – on the bare breasts of underage female fans invited into his dressing room one by one – he wouldn't have lasted five minutes.

I can recall feeling fairly disgusted when I found out what was going on, but it wouldn't have occurred to me, or any of us, to blow the whistle on him, he was the star of the show. If he got hauled off and the show closed we'd be out of work.

Chapter 5

SIX SHOWS A DAY

In 1955, Vivian Van Damm, a small, grey-haired, smartly-dressed, but rather doddery, old man who shuffled, was running the famous Windmill Theatre off Piccadilly Circus. The place had got its name from a windmill that stood on the site until the late eighteenth century and today is an erotic table-dancing club, but in Van Damm's day the Windmill had two claims to fame. One was it had remained open throughout World War II and the other was that it was the only legitimate place in London you could see a naked lady onstage. Despite the audience consisting almost exclusively of men in raincoats waiting to see a flash of nipple, it was a prestigious place to get a booking and pretty much anybody who became anybody had done a stint at the Windmill, especially comedians – Peter Sellers, Harry Secombe, Frankie Howerd, Benny Hill, Bruce Forsyth, Spike Milligan, Michael Bentine, Barry Cryer, Jimmy Edwards, Tony Hancock among them – but the occasional novelty or speciality act slipped in. Such as The King Brothers.

Everyone had to audition for "VD", as I'm afraid Van Damm was known, and we turned up to present our act on a cold grey morning in March. In a small area under the stage, already full of waiting auditionees, we changed into our KB outfits: shirts and clip-on bow ties and three different coloured jackets. Whilst doing so, I became fascinated by a man next to us in clown make-up and bright orange wig who had obviously been there for some time preparing for his act, and who seemed to have a rather complicated outfit. There had been much "pre-setting of things" going on, things that lit up or buzzed or beeped or whirled around or came out of his sleeves and pockets, hems, lapels and so on, and as his call came to go up onstage, he was frantically trying to tie on a pair of roller skates. Intrigued, I followed him up into the wings to watch his audition.

He handed his music to the pianist, made some last minute adjustments to his gadgetry, the piano struck up the intro of a song called *Happy Feet*, and the man started to tap dance on his roller skates but before he could open his mouth or indeed press any of his buttons, buzzers or levers, a voice from the stalls called out "Thank you! Next!" and the bewildered man exited stage left, Pagliacci-like, to no doubt spend the next hour having to take everything off again.

Our audition was fortunately more successful; not only did we get through our entire song without interruption, we were booked by VD for a six-week season to commence a month later. Our deal was £40 per week minus the booking agent's 10 per cent commission, and this was split among the three of us. We played six shows a day, starting at noon and finishing at 10pm, six days a week. That's 36 shows for £36. In other words, one pound per show, again to be split among the three of us, which in old money worked out at six shillings and eight pence each, per show. Once again, I was underage, so needed to get a special licence to perform. The management was particularly concerned because our act followed the Fan Dancer. Presumably you had to be at least 16 to see a lady naked.

The piano player would play an introduction, the blue velvet tabs would swing open, a rather camp tenor in a dinner suit standing at the side of the stage would start singing in a strangled voice, and a group of Windmill Lovelies as they were known, in flimsy flowing outfits, would glide on and move around, occasionally to the music. There were no complicated dance routines, the Lovelies were there solely to set the scene. After about a minute of this, the Fan Dancer, naked except for two ostrich-plume fans strategically positioned, would be "discovered" among the girls, and she too would sashay around vaguely to the music, all the while keeping her important regions covered by the plumes. As the song was reaching its end, she would pose in statuesque form upstage centre on a raised platform and, as the tenor in the dinner suit hit, or attempted to hit, the final note, the Fan Dancer would open her arms to reveal her naked form. Whereupon the tabs would instantly close. The whole thing was fairly tame by today's standards, but I wasn't allowed to see it.

Instead of being able to wait in the wings promising faithfully to look the other way or wear a bag over my head, I was made to stay up in our dressing room until I heard the tenor's closing bars, whereupon I would tear down three flights of stairs four steps at a time, frantically push a mini piano onstage and be ready at the keyboard, hands poised and smiling when the tabs opened on our act. Mike and Tony, meanwhile, would have strolled casually into position, having been legally lurking Off Stage Right getting eyefuls of forbidden parts.

As the curtain rose, the sound of silence which greeted The King Brothers was broken only by the crinkling of sandwiches being unwrapped, newspapers being brought out, and the squeak of theatre seats tipping up. As the shows at the Windmill were continuous, the audience could come and go as they pleased. If there were 10 or 15 people in at two in the afternoon you'd be lucky, and at least half of them would get up and leave as soon as they realised we weren't going to be nubile females with ostrich plumes. You got used to it. And besides, it wasn't just us that died a death, on the odd occasion a comedian got a laugh it was undoubtedly from some drunk who'd wandered in off the street and who was quickly shown the door. We were all there, really, only to fill a gap while the girls went up to the canteen on the top floor for a cigarette and a cup of tea – the same canteen, incidentally, which was also a favourite King Brother hangout, especially the younger newly licenced one with his eyes on stalks because the girls rarely bothered to wear anything more than skimpy see-through robes. I can only remember one, out of a total of 216 performances at the Windmill, that didn't end in stony silence for us.

It was the last show on a Saturday night. There had been a football match that day at Wembley Stadium between England and Scotland. Scotland had won, and their supporters, victorious in their tartan, descended on London, many of them packing themselves into the Windmill. They loved every act. They loved the comedian (Hugh Lloyd), they loved the cartoonist (Inky Williams), they – of course – loved the girls, but The King Brothers, for reasons we'll never know, sent them into a frenzy. The audience was on its feet, delirious. We took our bow to rapturous applause and whoops and whistles of acclaim and as we came off, the stage manager hastily pushed us back on for a second bow, something that had never happened before and we were in shock. In the heady rush to get back on stage, Mike slipped on the glass floor (the girls were lit from underneath) and fell onto his guitar, breaking it in half (and there you were thinking Pete Townshend invented this). The Scots assumed this was part of the act and gave Mike another standing ovation.

As if doing six shows a day at the Windmill wasn't enough, after our last one we'd drive over to Berkeley Square to the Astor Club, a seedy establishment frequented by "hostesses" (hookers), dancers, gangsters, and the occasional sozzled celebrity – and do two more shows, finishing around 2am. After which Mike would drive us in a Ford Zephyr back to Hornchurch. Every other Saturday we also managed to fit in an appearance on a children's television show called *Sugar & Spice*. You know, whenever I hear a performer complaining these days that eight shows a week is too demanding, claiming exhaustion or vocal strain, so " send on the understudy" – I think back on those Windmill days and wonder just how long any of them would have lasted with old Van Damm, ostrich plumes or not.

Chapter 6

NOW IS THE SUMMER
OF OUR DISCONTENT

The end of a long, wet, 20-week summer season, at the end of the long wet North Pier in Blackpool where the theatre was located, was crowned by a long, wet, pre-motorway drive home to Essex in a car not only full of King Brothers, suitcases, instruments and an actor friend named Bunny May, but one in which the windscreen wipers packed up 20 miles south of Blackpool. Through a crony at the Ford Motor Company (where else) my father had acquired for us a used Ford V8 Pilot Shooting Brake which had seen service for King George VI on the Sandringham Estate up in Norfolk. A bulky, cumbersome, wooden-bodied vehicle with a bench seat in front – driving it, according to Mike – who never allowed Tony nor me near the wheel – was like manoeuvering a tank, though how he'd know about tanks I don't know, having failed his medical for National Service (along with Tony and I – but that's another story).

The shooting brake had flick-out indicators, a windscreen that opened outwards, a wind-up starting handle like you see in old Buster Keaton films, and another handle inside on the dashboard for manually working the wipers, which I proceeded to do like a robot for the next seven-and-a-half hours of unrelenting rain all the way back to Chingford, where we still lived with our parents.

Variety performers based their year around getting a summer season. It guaranteed you employment for a good four months and you could still do the odd Sunday concert to boost your wage packet for the week.

Blackpool had been The King Brothers' fifth summer season in a row and, according to press cuttings, we'd already "startled Southport" with our "ability and stage presence", with me apparently "reducing the audience to tears" in my first acting role (as a poor urchin who wanted to buy flowers for his blind mother but only had thruppence) "exiting to thunderous applause and the sound of sobbing". In Weymouth, we "kept up the swift tempo of the show", in Southsea we appear to have been totally unmemorable, no cuttings exist, and in Morecambe, The King Brothers were "particularly well received for their smart musical numbers". What was not reported, was that the man who ran the theatre there made our lives, and everyone's, an utter misery.

The Central Pier Theatre, Morecambe was roughly the size of a village hall and the summer show was called *The Starlights*, as it had been every year for 12 years. It was comprised mostly of sketches and novelty acts, loosely linked, and I use the word "loosely" *very* loosely. Unlike Variety, however, this did entail rehearsing together as a unit, because you were all required to partici-

Mike, eldest King Brother, chaperone, and designated driver, posing, age 23, in front of our transport – a Ford V8 Pilot Shooting Brake that Dad secured for us and which hailed from King George VI's estate at Sandringham. Blackpool, 1958.

pate in the ensemble pieces in order to fill up the stage. You rehearsed the show for a week, played it for a week, during which you rehearsed a new show, eventually ending up with three shows in all, which were then rotated, after which your daytime was your own. In theory.

There were 15 "artistes", as we were known. Aly Wilson, a Scottish comedian, headed the bill (resort towns in the northwest of England used to attract a large contingent of Scots coming down during Wakes Week, which were holidays originally for mill workers seeking fun and frolics at the seaside). There was also Arthur Sumner, billed as Wilson's "admirable foil" and "a tenor of merit", a real tightwad who used to sneak sips of

Guinness from the glass of one of the musical clowns, Earl & Elgar, while they were onstage and then top up the glass with water. There was Howarth Nuttal, a baritone; Mary Redfern, a soprano; Lucy Loupé, a soubrette and, according to one review, "a real stalwart in the comedy sketches"; Juel Morrell, dancer and daughter of the producer; The Four Lovelies, one of whom had enormous knockers and to whom I was enormously attracted at age 15. Two piano players completed the cast, Arthur Jackson, a sweet old queen, and Ray Fenton, father of Kate, who later married actor Ian Carmichael. The producer was Eddie Morrell.

Now that name may mean little or nothing to you, but to those of us who performed on the Central Pier Morecambe in 1955, it conjures up mild feelings of retribution tantamount to wishing him hanged, drawn and quartered and seeing his head on a spike at the end of the pier. Small, red-faced, with a fiery temper, Eddie Morrell had a vindictive nature and ran the Pier Theatre with all the bonhomie that Stalin ran the gulags. Nobody in the show liked him, with the possible exception of his daughter Juel.

The contract he drew up for The Starlights company had a cunning clause that stipulated "matinées every day if wet or inclement", inclement being the key word here, for the summer of 1955 was one of the sunniest, hottest, driest summers on record. Cloudless skies stretched endlessly overhead and every day dawned clear and blue and promising. Picnics, outings, day trips to the countryside, all beckoned seductively. Alas, they were not to be. Comrade Morrell insisted that the whole company meet in the stalls of the Central Pier Theatre every day at one o'clock in the afternoon to await his verdict as to whether or not the weather was "inclement". He would arrive at least 45 minutes late.

We all sat there, waiting, in the stifling heat, stewing, and wondering where you could hire a hit man in Morecambe, and finally we'd hear the lobby doors behind us swing open. We'd then hear what very quickly became the intensely irritating tread of Morrell's feet as he slowly and deliberately made his way down the creaking aisle, pausing only to look out the side window of the auditorium, perhaps in the faint hope that a sudden monsoon had zeroed in on Morecambe Bay. He would then mount the steps to the stage, face the assembled gathering of hugely-pissed-off performers, and pause. Eventually, and with a look of acute disappointment at being unable to detain us any longer, he would make the inevitable announcement in his whiny, nasal, high-pitched voice.

Programme from our summer season at Weymouth's Alexandra Gardens Theatre, 1956. It claims to be a "London West End Production" but it never went near the place. I'm sure I would have noticed.

"Due to the weather conditions, there will be no matinée…" and before he could say the word "today", the entire Starlights company would be on its feet and out the door and into the baking sunshine. Morrell did this every day for 12 weeks, and every day for 12 weeks our summer hopes and dreams were shattered – particularly my chance to to see the Fourth Lovely in her bikini.

The following summer, Frank Earl, one of the musical clowns, picked up the sign that said "Matinées Every Day If Wet Or Inclement" and hurled it off the pier, then thumped Morrell, knocking him off, too. Sadly, the tide was in and I believe he survived.

Blackpool Summer Season, 1958, on the other hand, was a summer Eddie Morrell would have loved. It rained incessantly for 20 weeks.

The pier was and still is a quarter-of-a- mile long with virtually no shelter along it, and the theatre was situated at the far end. You would arrive at the stage door drenched and windswept, and breathless from running the gauntlet of holiday-makers intent on intercepting you, people who were either on their way to see the show or had already seen it.

"You'd better be good tonight, we're paying bluddy good money to see you!"

"Ee, you're a lot smaller than you look on't telly!"

David Nixon of TV's *What's My Line*, one of the stars of the summer show, had the misfortune of being not only extremely tall but in possession of a very recognisable bald head, so was an especially easy target even while dashing down the wet pier. He loathed being accosted and used an assortment of disguises to avoid being recognised – hats, wigs, false noses, whiskers, spectacles – but they never worked and he'd arrive at the stage door seething.

"Saw t'show last night. Din't think much of it," I heard someone once say to him.

Despite the foul weather and David's occasional foul mood, it was a happy company. Billy Dainty, Edmund Hockridge, Joan Regan, David Nixon were all delightful, also some identical spinster twins in their fifties who drove a vintage car round the stage (there must have been more to the act), whose names I've forgotten. You'd all meet up at the theatre in the morning to check for post, then go off and have a coffee, probably head to the cinema in the afternoon, and most nights after the show all go out for a bite to eat together. Sundays were the same apart from not having a show to do.

And then, it happened. During a chance outing to the Open Championship at Royal Lytham. My brother Tony and I discovered a game called golf. And from then on, there were never enough hours in the day.

Fortunately, golf, as everyone knows, at least in this country, is one of those versatile sports with which one can while away one's leisure time quite contentedly in almost any weather, all one needs is one's waterproofs, fortitude, and a degree of insanity in the family, and I will not, at this time, discuss in detail my birdie at the 6th at Hoylake, or indeed take you through every round I've ever played, hole by hole. That would be more my brother Tony's field and this is my book, not his, but let me just say that having a hobby, and one that can be enjoyed anywhere, made life on the road away from home just that little more bearable.

While golf was the high point of our summer in Blackpool, the low point was the accommodation my father had arranged for us. He rarely got involved in any of the mundane, practical aspects of our career, being much more adept at pointing out our names on posters

67

to anyone passing and letting them know we were his lads, but when he found out that an old school friend of his named Harry Ashton, a man who for once had nothing to do with the Ford Motor Company, owned a small hotel on the north shore called The Atlantic, a typical seaside boarding house, Dad got in touch. It was already fully booked out but as a favour to Mum and Dad, Harry said he'd find room for us for the season and do us a special deal. Dad patted himself on the back.

The deal turned out to be very special indeed. It consisted of cramming a third single bed into a small room that had two already in it. Harry Ashton charged us £9 per week each, making it a total of £27 for the room. We found out the normal charge was £18. A month after we moved in, a friend of the King family, Mike McDonnell, a golf journalist, came up to cover the Open Championship, couldn't find a place to stay, asked us if there was by chance any spare room at The Atlantic, we asked Harry, Harry said yes of course, crammed another single bed into our already tight accommodation, and ended up getting £36 per week for a room you had to walk across beds in order to get in or out of.

The Atlantic's other main attraction was the breakfast gong situated directly outside our door and which was energetically struck, presumably by Harry, to announce the two morning sittings, the first at 7.30am, the second 45 minutes later – or roughly the time it took us all to stop vibrating.

As another great favour, Harry suggested we boys might like to borrow his caravan for a Sunday overnight near Windermere up in the Lake District. He said we looked tired and needed a break, which was true, but why the three of us, who spent every moment of every day and night together would even contemplate spending our one day off together, I can't begin to fathom. But we did, primarily to escape The Atlantic, I imagine.

First thing on a wet Sunday morning, Tony, Mike and I set off in King George VI's old V-8 Pilot Shooting Brake to make our way north to Wordsworth country intending to wander lonely as a cloud that floats on high o'er vales and hills, but all we saw was blinding rain, no sign of bleedin' daffodils. Nor, in fact, Lake Windermere. Hours of winding roads later, we managed to locate the caravan, deep in the woods.

It was at first sight something of a disappointment; it looked like a small wooden box on wheels. Nevertheless, we made a dash for it through the torrential downpour and in no time at all made the discovery that the inside was even less inviting than the outside. The green interior walls, which we'd thought were painted, turned out to be stripes of mould and mildew, there was no loo or kitchen and, not surprisingly, it was cold.

After much fiddling with valves and matches, one of us managed to get the Calor gas heater lit, whereupon we unwrapped our cheese sandwiches, got out a pack of cards, and squeezed ourselves around a fold-down table in front of a wrinkled plastic window down which water was furiously sheeting, to enjoy our holiday. Within minutes we were overcome by gas fumes and had to open the door. The rain poured in. We lasted perhaps 45 minutes, after which, by unanimous decision, any plans for an overnight stay were abandoned. We piled back into the shooting brake, set off into the mist and, once we'd understood we were *on* the main road and had stopped looking for it, returned post haste to The Atlantic, which had suddenly taken on all the allure of the Beverly Hills Hotel.

Another few weeks there, however, was enough to

cure us of this mental aberration and we checked out, moving into a large house that singer Edmund Hockridge had rented, along with his wife Jackie, dancer Terry Donovan, who later became and still is Mrs. Barry Cryer, and actor-comedian Jack Douglas who, by the way, later went on to give one of the least convincing portrayals of Long John Silver in the history of *Treasure Island* that I've ever seen, in a musical version that Willis Hall and I had been commissioned to write for Birmingham Repertory Theatre (see Chapter 21).

Harry Ashton was not best pleased by our departure apparently, and complained to my father that we had let him down and ruined his summer. Mum, Dad and our sister Moira had come up to see us in Blackpool, and I know stayed at The Atlantic too, but I assume in their own room, because I'm pretty sure I would have remembered had Harry stuffed three more beds into ours.

Chapter 7

THREE ENGLISHMEN ABROAD

Some time later in 1955, Denny Boyce, a local Ilford bandleader who billed himself as "Denny Boyce – The Band of Your Choice!", had stepped into the illustrious shoes of Mr. Ron Sensier, head-gasket-fitter of the Ford Motor Company, to become the new manager of The King Brothers and, thanks to him, we spent a thoroughly miserable Christmas and New Year away from our family, shivering and starving on an air base in Germany.

"Denny Boyce – The Band of Your Choice!" had negotiated for us a month's tour of US Air Force bases. Mike was 20, Tony was 18, and I, by then at 16, was for some reason still underage and needed to secure a special magistrate's licence to perform. It was our first time out of England.

Excited, but nervous, we bid our farewells – a kiss for Mum and little Moira, a handshake for Dad – and in mid-December boarded a train with our luggage, the double bass and Mike's guitar. We then boarded another train and then a boat. Arriving at Ostend in the dark, we found our way to the railway station, onto yet another train, and arrived in Frankfurt as dawn broke on a freezing Monday morning, where we had to wait for a connection to Kaiserslautern, our final destination. We were directed to a railway waiting area designated for non-Germans.

Almost as soon as we'd sat down, an American woman leapt up and screamed.

"I've been robbed! He took my purse!"

She pointed to a scruffy young man running out the door. Through the station window we watched as two German policemen – looking like SS guards in helmets, long black leather coats, and jackboots – gave chase. They grabbed the man, threw him to the platform and, while one held him down, the other kicked him again and again and again. This was our welcome to Germany, 10 years after the war.

Some hours later – cold, hungry, tired and still somewhat shaken – we stumbled off a military bus at the air base just outside Kaiserslautern, then home to the largest US military community outside the United States and where it soon became apparent that no one had ever heard of The King Brothers, let alone expected us, nor knew quite what to do with us. There had been no directives preceding us from "Denny Boyce – The Band of Your Choice!", warm and cosy back in England, and whose final instructions to us had been that we'd be met, provided with funds, and everything would be taken care of. We had only small change in our pockets and no way of contacting anyone. Eventually, some kind military man found us accommodation in the officers' quarters. As we were unpacking, there was a knock on the door.

In walked a familiar face, Billy "Uke" Scott, a performer with whom we had worked precisely once (he

The King Brothers

Personal Manager:
DENNY BOYCE,
322 Streatham High Road,
London, S.W.16

STReatham 1084/5

The smiling King Brothers circa 1955, as yet unaware that our new personal manager, Denny Boyce – an Ilford band leader who billed himself as "Denny Boyce – The Band of Your Choice!" – would prove to be somewhat of a disappointment.

73

played the ukulele and sang comic songs, not unlike George Formby) but whom we greeted almost tearfully, as if he were part of the family. Billy invited us into his quarters, which were warmer than ours, and where he was in the process of having breakfast, which he continued to prepare, in front of us, and then eat, in front of us, without offering us any. Three pairs of eyes watched his every move, dog-like, as his hand went from table to mouth.

After he'd consumed his delicious-smelling boiled eggs, hot toast and tea, Billy "Uke" asked if we'd like a lift into town – I think we wanted to get stamps for postcards home to say what a good time we were having or possibly make a plea for a Red Cross parcel. He pulled the car over to drop us in the middle of some Platz or other, turned, and, unbelievably, asked for money for the petrol. Even more unbelievably, we gave it to him, our last coins. For the record, Billy "Uke" Scott died in 2004. I didn't go to his funeral. I was worried I'd find a bill waiting for 40 litres of unleaded when I got there.

What "Denny Boyce – The Band of Your Choice!" also hadn't told us was that once we arrived at Kaiserslautern air base, we'd have to audition. In a vast, echoey, what appeared to be aircraft hangar, we joined a group of 30 or 40 hopefuls of various nationalities. In front of us sat an undulating mass of big-bellied, cigar-smoking, bourbon-swilling US Air Force master sergeants, all looking like less genial versions of Rod Steiger's redneck cop in *In The Heat Of The Night*. The audition process that followed was what I imagine a Saturday morning cattle market in Abilene might be like.

You'd finish your act, the sergeants would loudly negotiate among themselves as to: a) whether they thought you were any good; and b) if you were, who would have who for what date.

"Hey no way you sonofabitch! *I* want the magic guy for Sunday, you already got that asshole on the banjo!"

The King Brothers sang a song called *Mobile Alabama* which must have struck a chord with the Rod Steigers because afterwards we became the subject of much-heated bartering and for the first time since we'd left Hornchurch, felt very wanted.

Our forthcoming appearances were not due to start until the 26th of December, three days later, which meant we still had no money, even for food. Christmas dinner was celebrated in a sparsely- populated soup kitchen on the base. We shared a table with a homesick and increasingly lachrymose NCO and three taciturn, stony-faced army privates nursing hangovers.

Our tour consisted of one- night stands at US military bases around Bavaria. Lest you conjure up a fairy tale Disneyland castle picture of Bavaria, you should know that Bavaria, in the winter of 1955, was still recovering from the war, and had, from what we could see out of the bus window, all the appeal of a construction site in Gdansk.

Secondly, unlike the acts one worked with in Twice Nightly Variety back in England, our co-performers here, with few exceptions, were only there to escape from something even more unpleasant somewhere else, they might be on the run from the tax man or ex-wives, some were draft-dodgers, and one was almost certainly hiding from his own past.

"The Great Alex", as he billed himself, juggled Indian clubs. Blonde, blue-eyed, of medium build, he kept to himself and never said a word to anyone. The first time we shared a dressing room with him was in Heidelberg. He acknowledged our hellos with a curt nod and turned away. As he stripped off his street clothes to change into his juggling clothes, we saw, briefly, before he quickly pulled his shirt down, a tattoo under his left arm: the gothic lettering of the Waffen-SS was unmistakable.

The shows themselves fell into a routine. You'd arrive somewhere, have a burger and a Coke in the PX, get changed in somebody's office next to a mute tattooed Nazi, go on and do your 20 minutes on a makeshift stage where occasionally the piano had been tuned, then get back on the bus to slip and slide on icy roads all the way back to Kaiserslautern.

The audiences, mostly military men with the odd military wife thrown in, seemed grateful to see pretty much anything, but give them a bit of boogie woogie and they'd go wild. Sometimes too wild. We spent New Year's Eve performing, or attempting to, at an enlisted men's club on a US Army base at Würzburg.

Whoever had organised the evening didn't want us to appear until just before midnight so, after we'd changed in the unheated storeroom they'd provided, we hung around drinking coffee for an hour-and-a-half. I don't know what time the party had started but by the time we made our entrance, the all-male audience was thoroughly sozzled. Loud and raucous, everyone seemed to be shouting and swearing or falling off their chairs. We made our way to our instruments. Nobody seemed particularly interested in our arrival. Mike plugged in his electric guitar, we took our positions, I played the intro and we began our jolly opener.

WE WANNA SAY HELLO!
WE WANNA SEE YOU SMILE!

A soldier staggered onto the dance floor in front of us, brandishing a knife, but not at us, so we carried on.

WE'RE HERE TO ENTERTAIN YOU ONCE AGAIN!

Someone lurched towards him, a big black guy, then someone got up, a big white guy, then a couple more big black guys, then more big white guys and within seconds a violent race war had broken out in the room. Chairs went flying, tables were overturned, bottles were smashed; suddenly blood and broken glass were everywhere. The King Brothers played on.

WE WANNA DO THE LITTLE THINGS
WE USED TO DO BEFORE!

MPs with raised batons now stormed in, bashing heads right and left as they bulldozed around the room and no sooner was one fracas suppressed than three others broke out. In the melee, Mike's amplifier lead was yanked out.

Still we played on, rather like the band on the *Titanic*, until finally somebody had the presence of mind to lean over the piano and scream "For Chrissakes, get the fuck outta here!", which seemed like good advice and which we then proceeded to do, sharpish.

The thought of another three weeks entertaining troops became less appealing by the hour, but we had a contract, so we soldiered on to Weisbaden, Mannheim, Ramstein, all the steins – all of us desperately homesick, cold, and fed up. In retrospect, it might have been sensible to drink ourselves senseless every night after the show but we never thought of it. No groupies crowded round either, to fight over us. Mike once attempted to impress a local fräulein who'd spent time working as an au pair in Birmingham, but he gave up when he couldn't cope with the impenetrable Brummie Bavarian accent she'd acquired.

With bandleader/agent "Denny Boyce – The Band of Your Choice!" – in The Ilford Pictorial. *The photo was taken in December of 1955, before we left on a tour of USAF bases in Germany which "Denny Boyce – The Band of Your Choice!" had arranged. Had it been taken upon our return, chances are he wouldn't be in the photo, since we would have been hard pressed not to put three pairs of hands around his throat.*

Possibly the highlight of my entire trip was buying a bottle of Old Spice aftershave in the PX. I'd heard about it, but you couldn't buy it in England.

When we arrived back in the UK it was mid-afternoon. We went straight from the airport (our first flight – almost as exciting as the aftershave) to the Granada Theatre in East Ham to do a week's Variety, followed by another flight, this time to Amsterdam to perform on TV in honour of Princess Beatrix's 18th birthday, which happened to coincide with Tony's 19th. Tony sang *Happy Birthday* to Beatrix, in Dutch, which he doesn't speak, and which I am sorry to say wasn't recorded. Think Marilyn Monroe serenading JFK, but with not as sexy a dress.

According to an article headed "BUSY AGENT!" in the February 1956 *Romford Recorder*, "Denny Boyce – The Band of Your Choice But Not Necessarily Mine", spent much of his time, quote, "meeting The King Brothers and seeing them off again at London Airport!" unquote, but this can't possibly be true, since anyone who'd been responsible for the Deluxe Premier Tour of Germany that we'd just experienced would have kept well out of our way.

Chapter 8

HOWARD'S END

The ultimate job, the dream job of every artiste who'd ever appeared on the Variety circuit, was to play the great London Palladium. It was run by the all-powerful impresario, Mr. Val Parnell. Wherever you were playing, hearing that he was in the audience that night was the equivalent today of learning that, say, Cameron Mackintosh was out front. Parnell caught our act at the Finsbury Park Empire. He didn't come backstage, in fact I'm not entirely sure we even knew he was in, which would have saved having to be nervous about it, but afterwards Parnell got in touch with our agent and, miraculously, one month later "The King Brothers - TV's Teenage Stars!" were up there on the bill at the London Palladium alongside Howard Keel, comedians Harry Worth and Tommy Trinder (who was assisted by Anne Hart, later to become Mrs. Ronnie Corbett), the American tap dancing Nicholas Brothers, Evie and Joe Slack, who must have done something but I can't remember what, adagio dancers Les Curibas, "International Wizard" Richiardi Junior, an illusionist who levitated (never to be seen again) and the George Carden Dancers.

It was an unbelievable thrill for three young kids from Hornchurch.

Howard Keel was then one of the biggest movie stars in the world. He had a superb stage act and was such a draw that even before we'd opened, all performances had sold out, all 2,300 seats, every night, for the entire two week run. He was friendly and encouraging and terribly kind to us, in fact everyone was. Tommy Trinder compered the show, and would always call us back on stage for another bow, getting a round of applause for himself in the process with a topical joke about the "KBs" on our jackets being the same initials as Khruschev and Bulganin, the Soviet leaders currently visiting London. It was only marginally more amusing than Dad's observation about our "KBs" matching the name of his new Kolster-Brandes television, but we stood there in the bright lights, reacting appropriately with big grins, every night, as if we'd never heard it before. You learned quickly.

The heaving mass of fans waiting for Howard Keel at the Palladium stage door after every show was my first taste of real hero-worship. Unlike the heavily-disguised David Nixon scurrying along the North Pier in Blackpool with his head down, Howard didn't wear hats or wigs or false noses to avoid his fans, on the contrary, he welcomed them, always graciously, and always stayed around after the show giving autographs until every last book had been signed. It was a fine lesson in how to treat one's public and I've tried never to forget it. Not that I've experienced a plethora of heaving masses of fans myself except perhaps years later when a television theme of mine went "gold" in Sweden, but my instincts

The London Palladium theatre programme, April 1956, starring one of my then heroes, Howard Keel.

anyhow are to be pleasant to people. Last week, for instance, I was stopped in the local Tesco's by a small, stout, elderly woman with white hair.

"I'll bet you don't remember me, do you?" she said, which I didn't, even when she said her name was Bebe.

"Great Yarmouth?" she prompted, eyes twinkling. "1959? Under the pier? The tide took my shoes?"

"Bebe!" I said, not having a clue. Gradually, a picture of a pretty blonde with great legs came into focus. Of course, I thought! Bebe Merchant! The dancer in Great Yarmouth. Lovely creature. I was about to say, "How is she?" when realisation hit. This dear old woman was Bebe?

"You look... fantastic!" I said.

She beamed and I went home thinking, Christ, isn't this age business dreadful, and congratulated myself, somewhat prematurely, that at least it hadn't yet caught up with *me* – she'd recognised me instantly! An hour later I went past the hall mirror and saw the big name tag still pinned to my lapel from a local charity thing I'd done earlier that said "DENIS KING – COMPOSER AND FORMER KING BROTHER".

The second most important thing to learn about show business, after Be Nice To Your Fans And Anyone You've Rolled Around Under A Pier With, is not to get too carried away by success, to understand that within the short space of 48 hours it is possible to plunge from the dizzying heights of Howard Keel and the London Palladium to the Palace Theatre, Hull, sharing a dressing room with "Marqueez and his Chattering Chimps" and "Kalanag the Wonder Man, He Fills the Stage with Flags!"

I have no idea what ever happened to Marqueez or Kalanag or how they ended their days, but thanks to a somewhat surreal conversation I had, following friend and humorist Alan Coren's memorial service at St. Bride's, Fleet Street a few years ago, I do happen to know where Howard Keel is. Or at least a part of him. Roughly. As a group of us walked from St. Bride's to a nearby pub for refreshments, I overheard the following:

"Oh, that reminds me! I must do something with Howard Keel's ashes!"

I mulled this over then turned, intrigued, and addressed the speaker, the wife of an actor friend.

"Sorry to interrupt, but what did you just say?"

She went on to explain that when Howard died in November 2004 it had been his wish that some of his ashes be scattered at the Theatre Royal, Drury Lane, the site of his first London stage appearance in 1947. Apparently, Mrs. Keel never got round to it, or didn't know how to do it, or something, anyhow about three years later she entrusted our actor friend with a box partially-full of Howard. It seems this well-known actor and Howard had played golf together up in Cheshire once and that's why the actor got the ashes – a connection I don't completely understand – but in any event, the actor, to my knowledge, although he has been meaning to, has yet to scatter Howard's ashes at Drury Lane and, from what I can gather, is none too sure as to where, exactly, in the house, or in which cupboard, Howard has been placed for safekeeping. Which explains why Howard was on their "To Do" list.

I would like to take this opportunity to instruct my wife or son or anyone I've played golf with that as far as *my* ashes are concerned, I have no wish whatsoever to be scattered at the Finsbury Park Empire. Apart from anything else I believe it's now a branch of Marks & Spencer.

Chapter 9

"THE SINGING GROUP THAT SIZZLES!"

When we weren't on the road doing summer seasons, Variety tours, concerts or TV appearances, The King Brothers could usually be found at home in Essex rehearsing new material in our parents' front room. Prior to our first recording contract, we chose our repertoire ourselves, usually standards and current hits like *Rock Around The Clock* but also the odd novelty song like *The Hawaiian War Chant*, which none of us now remember choosing, or at least won't own up to it. It began like this:

TA AH-TOO-ALA AH-TOO-ALA AH-WAHEELA
AH-HOO-WANA-LA-AH-PEE-LEE-CO
AH-LOO-ALA TA AH-TOO-ALA AH AH AH-TOO-ALA
ANA-LA PO-WEE-A PAH-OO-LAH-EE
OOO! OOO! OOO!

...and continued in much the same catchy vein.

We had no idea what we were singing about and having just Googled the song, it appears we might have been singing the wrong lyrics anyway, but the audience at the Sheffield Empire certainly never noticed, for according to the local paper they "went berserk", when we launched into it, especially when we donned crepe paper Hawaiian garlands for the second chorus. Quite extraordinary. Whether or not this was due to something special in the water up there, I have no idea. Perhaps Sheffield is twinned with Honolulu.

Rehearsals at home were, as a rule, not much fun. Mike would sleep late, wake up in a bad mood and come downstairs spoiling for an argument, which was never long in coming, primarily because Tony knew how to push Mike's buttons, and this he did, almost gleefully, whenever he had the chance, knowing that Mike had a short fuse and might explode at anything, that even bad weather could set him off (and still does). Mike considered himself the leader of the pack, which he indeed was in the early days by virtue of his age, but he carried this attitude right through to the break-up of the act. I tried not to take sides in any brotherly disputes, in the vain hope that Mike would see reason and calm would prevail – but more often than not, despite whatever I'd say or not say, I'd find myself in the firing line.

Returning home one Monday morning after a late Sunday night concert in Liverpool, Mike at the wheel of the Ford station wagon and Tony, as usual, asleep in the back seat, somewhere south of Birmingham we came to a roundabout.

"We turn left here," I said, helpfully.

"No, it's straight on."

"I'm sorry, but it's definitely left. We're not going to

The King Brothers performing on The Rolf Harris Show *in the early 1960s. I don't know whose idea the hats were, certainly not mine.*

Wales."

"Don't tell me!" Mike snapped. I insisted I was right. "You say that again, and you can get out of the car!"

I said it again. There was a screech of brakes. Mike leaned across, pushed open the passenger door, and ordered me out. I got out. He drove off. It was 7am. Heavy lorries rumbled by. I didn't know where I was.

Ten minutes passed. The familiar station wagon reappeared, pulled up, and the door was flung open.

"Get in!" Mike said, without looking at me. I did, and we drove back to the roundabout, turned left (correctly) and drove home to Essex without a further word being exchanged and certainly not an apology. Tony slept through the entire episode.

Luckily for me, even though our rehearsal process was somewhat determined by Mike's mood at the time, the one area in which he felt out of his depth was music, and here he would bow to my judgement. For every new number we wanted to include in our act, I'd first of all knock out the melody on the piano and work out the vocal parts, which we'd all then practise. Next, I'd write an easy guitar part for Mike, a marginally more difficult bass part for Tony, which they would then both practise until it wasn't too bad, whereupon we'd put it all together and rehearse it until Mike stormed off in a temper or Mum called us to lunch. Or both, as can be illustrated by the Salmon and Parsley Sauce Incident.

It began one lunch-time by Tony continuing to do whatever it was he had been doing to irritate Mike, all the way to the dining table. Mum bustled in, set our steaming plates in front of us (or perhaps the steam was coming from Mike's ears) and returned to the kitchen. The three of us began to eat. Tony said something, Mike snapped something back, I interjected a conciliatory something else, and suddenly a plate of tinned salmon, mashed potatoes, peas and parsley sauce came hurtling in my direction. I ducked, Tony ducked, the plate hit the wall, and Mike's lunch – his favourite, incidentally – slid slowly down the wallpaper in a slippery mess just as Mum came back in from the kitchen. She gasped, horrified, then her gaze fell on Mike and his vacant placemat. Now, Mum would argue black was white as far as Mike was concerned, you could never criticise him in front of her – but for one shining moment in the newly-decorated dining room, his position as Number One Son hovered briefly on "Ever-So-Slightly Precarious".

Of course, thinking about it all now, the three of us probably got on about as well as any brothers that close in age would, probably better, given our unusual situation of being in one another's hair 24 hours a day. No argument, however, was worth breaking up the act for. Without the act, we'd have nothing, and we knew it. So we just got on with it. We knew that to survive you had to take a deep breath and forgive and forget and learn how to override petty grievances, and to apologise whenever necessary (unless, of course, you were Mike).

The aim of every musical act was (and still is) to land a recording contract. I'd like to say it was also The King Brothers' burning ambition, but I don't recall us thinking much about it, I certainly didn't. At 17, I was almost solely preoccupied with getting Brigitte Bardot into my bed although, of course, I didn't technically know her, and the likelihood of running into her in our Weymouth digs was remote. (My love affair with golf would not come until a few years later, at which time I imagined Brigitte and me playing a round together. Golf, that is.)

The King Brothers' recording career – just happened.

Record producer and songwriter Norman Newell, who had once been a bus driver in Hornchurch, was in the television studio audience the night we were appearing on *The Gracie Fields Show*. He thought we had potential as recording artists, and arranged for us to make a trial record. It was only of slightly better quality than the acetate one Mike and I had once made in a booth for two shillings, but Norman was pleased enough with the result to get us a contract with Parlophone Records. Our first single was a song called *Marianne*, a kind of calypso tune, which we recorded at the legendary Abbey Road Studios. We had a modest success with it, at least enough to get us noticed by the record-buying public. Norman then found us a song called *A White Sport Coat (And A Pink Carnation)*.

This became our first "hit" and got to number six in the charts. Our Parlophone royalty was only one and a half pence per record, just over half a pence in today's money, but Mum and Dad were ecstatic. Every time our "hit" was played, Mum, who must have had the radio on permanently, would phone us down in Southsea where we were appearing for the summer, to tell us she'd heard it again, and my father went off to work no doubt dreaming of a new model soon to hit the Ford assembly line: the Kingmobile!

Norman Newell found us more hit singles. *Mais Oui, In The Middle Of An Island, Doll House* and our biggest success, *Standing On The Corner*. Suddenly we were celebrities. It was goodbye Pop, White & Stagger and hello Judy Garland. Suddenly we were working with stars. Sarah Vaughan. Frankie Vaughan. Sophie Tucker. Bobby Darin. Eddie Fisher. Shirley Bassey. Jerry Colonna. Kay Starr. Gloria de Haven. Harry Secombe. We signed with a new agency, the Delfont Organisation. Our income increased. Not by much, but I could finally afford that snazzy dark blue and purple pinstripe Italian bum-freezer jacket from Cecil Gee in Shaftesbury Avenue I'd been longing for. Life was good. We were invited onto Royal Variety shows. We got fan mail (which my mother answered). We had a fan club, with membership at five shillings a year (25p), which entitled you to meet "a

The King Brothers make the Hit Parade in the New Musical Express, *1961.*

welcoming King Brother" (rarely Mike) backstage after a show. Tony and I would toss a coin and the loser would resignedly descend to the stage door to endure 10 minutes of silly giggling girls who had absolutely nothing to say and we couldn't wait to get rid of them. (So much for our lesson from Howard Keel on how to treat fans.)

Having a record in the Top Ten guaranteed not only more work but requests for personal appearances. Invitations to openings, closings, unveilings, ribbon cuttings, flooded in from all over. Madrid! Brussels! Cologne! Venice! Lisbon! Eastleigh (!) Where I see under the headline "Kings Meet Queens!", The King Brothers provided "additional carnival attraction" when we judged a beauty contest (and selected a Mrs. Griffin). We seemed to have had some event somewhere every day that entailed a jacket and tie and a clean shirt. Mum did our laundry – by hand, no washing machine – and all our ironing, and the cooking, and the cleaning, and kept the accounts, and I'm sorry to say that, like our father, we were happy to be waited on hand and foot. We gave

Hitting the Big Time in Eastleigh, 1956.

interviews and had our pictures taken. If we bought a new car or if Mike took a girl to a film premiere, it made the papers. We contributed a recipe for onion soup to the *Dudley Herald*, modelled for easy-knit golfing sweaters for *Woman's Mirror*, and in a TV magazine article entitled "They've Been Rockin'!" I was described as "diminutive Denis" three times. We were hot. "The Singing Group That Sizzles!"

We'd arrived.

Norman Newell had made it all happen. We remained friends over the years and he produced the cast albums for two musicals of mine. Likeable, gay, and friendly, Norman – whose name, to his amusement, was sometimes misprinted in the papers as "Normal Newell" – was full of ideas, always enthusiastic, always supportive, easy to work with, and I remember him with huge affection.

He was also a gifted lyricist. One of his biggest hits was *A Portrait Of My Love*, Matt Monro's first chart success, and he was especially proud of being nominated for an Academy Award for a song called *More*, a piece of information he managed to insert into almost every conversation, wherever he was, whatever was being discussed, be it the Cuban missile crisis, Idi Amin, or the best route to the North Circular.

I try to think of Norman whenever I get depressed. I conjure up an image of him, head on the block, being asked if he has any last words before the axe falls.

"I wrote *More*, you know," he says, twinkling.

"No shit?" says the executioner. Then WHACK.

Chapter 10

THE GERRY'S CLUB YEARS

Being "diminutive" is, of course, not always a bad thing (as long as I can remember where my tall Nordic wife keeps the stepladder) as I'm sure comedian Ronnie Corbett would be the first to admit.

The Buckstone Club, behind the Theatre Royal, Haymarket, was a popular actors' hang-out in the late Fifties and early Sixties and chiefly notable, for me, as my first encounter with Ronnie, then an unemployed actor working as a part-time barman. It is my recollection that he stood on a box behind the bar but perhaps I just like the image. With the exception of the delightful, departed Dudley Moore, Ronnie is the only friend I have who's more diminutive than I (and so even if I didn't like him I'd enjoy standing next to him).

A year or so after the Buckstone encounter we found ourselves spending the summer together at the London Palladium in Harry Secombe's show *Let Yourself Go!*, I with my brothers, and Ronnie doing walk-on parts in sketches with Harry. We all became close friends. Ronnie at the time was living in a slightly tatty ground-floor flat on Camden Road and drove a second-hand Austin Healy Sprite that had a large hole in the floor. I was riding with him in it one rainy Sunday night not far from the one-way system at Swiss Cottage in north London, when a large Mark 10 Jaguar cut in front of us, forcing Ronnie to brake sharply.

"Bastard!" he shouted, as the Jag sped off. "Did you see that? I'm going to get him!"

The Sprite shot forward and we roared up the Finchley Road as if it were the home straight at Brands Hatch, bouncing and rattling along, zooming through puddles, water erupting through the hole in the floor (I kept my feet on the dashboard) and to Ronnie's delight, we spotted the offending Jag stopped at the next red light. With a squeal of brakes the Sprite pulled up behind it.

"Right!" said Ronnie, and then, I think you could say to my horror, he flung open his door and leapt out.

Through the rain-streaked windscreen – as I sank lower into my seat – I could see him banging on the Jag driver's window, shaking his fist in anger. The driver's door opened, and out stepped the biggest man I'd ever seen in my life, wearing a camel-hair coat, and with a face that would have sent me scurrying straight back to the Sprite, had it ever in a million years occurred to me to leave it in the first place.

The man looked down at Ronnie with an expression of utter astonishment, then burst out laughing.

Ronnie, unfazed, hopping up and down, purple with rage, jabbed his finger accusingly at about level with the man's belt buckle and continued his tirade as the man turned and beckoned into the Jag, whereupon three more large men in camel-hair coats stepped out. They too regarded Ronnie with curiosity, rather as a child might observe a funny little caterpillar, then all four burst into almost uncontrollable laughter, which only infuriated Ronnie more. Chuckling and shaking their heads as if they couldn't wait to get home to tell the story to their gangster friends, they then all piled back into the Jag and sped off as the lights changed.

Ronnie, hands on hips, regarded the disappearing tail lights for a moment then marched back to the Sprite and got in, bedraggled, soaked and dripping (not that it made any difference to the upholstery).

"Huh! They won't do that again!"

He slammed the door with a sense of accomplishment then put the car into gear and we rattled on down the Finchley Road.

I didn't ride with Ronnie again until 2005, after actor Denis Quilley's memorial service, by which time Ronnie was driving a Rolls Royce with no hole in the floor and, I'm pleased to say, we arrived at the National Theatre without incident.

In what came to be known as The Swinging Sixties, the quest for the perfect female companion was ongoing, but in the meantime, one was more than happy to settle for a nice bit of "crumpet" and crumpet, in London at least, was not especially difficult to acquire. One evening playing table tennis at the Pheasantry Club, an actors' club on Wellington Road, I suggested, purely as a joke, to Gerry Grant, a singer friend, that whoever won the next match would get to spend the night with the barmaid, a tall, voluptuous, ex-Bluebell showgirl named Miranda. To our amazement, and considerable delight, Miranda laughingly said "Sure! Why not?" to our proposal, as if we'd just asked if she'd like a packet of crisps, whereupon I played table tennis like a man possessed, trounced Gerry, and carried my prize home (actually she carried me).

Home at the time was a small studio flat in South Kensington. At the age of 24 I had moved out of the family home in Buckhurst Hill, Essex (which my brothers and I had bought for our parents) into what in my mind was going to be the perfect bachelor pad, the ultimate "des res" with beautiful girls tripping in and out as if through a revolving door – why, I'd be turning them away there'd be so many! And to cap it all, from my second-floor window vantage point right on the Fulham Road, I would not only be able to watch the wonderful world of high heels and miniskirts tottering by, but also inhale the heady scent of city life, happy, fulfilled, and basking gloriously in the knowledge that London was the centre of the universe and I was right at its heart. Helped by Mum and Dad, I moved into my second-floor front studio flat at 216 Fulham Road SW10 on the 22nd of November, 1963 – the same day that JFK was assassinated. Not a good omen.

I had a piano, a single divan that became a bed at night, a chest of drawers, and an armchair. I'd brought a kettle with me, a portable radio, a black-and-white TV, and a Goblin Teasmade that some stage-door fan had given me, and which I placed next to the bed, thinking it a marvellously convenient idea and the perfect way to wake up, and couldn't wait to try it.

On my first night as Jack The Lad Around Town, I stayed in, too tired to go out. I made up the divan bed, then remembered the Goblin Teasmade, which took forever to set up, primarily trying to make sense of the directions, and I ran back and forth from my tiny kitchen with water, then tea, then packets of sugar, then milk, spoon, cup and saucer and so on, and finally, after one last check, went to bed, exhausted but content. I woke the next morning just before the Goblin's timer was due to go off, and lay there, in my new divan bed, counting the seconds, looking forward to turning my head on the pillow and being able to watch my morning tea being made.

The timer beeped, I heard the machine click on, and looked round expectantly with a smile, just in time to see boiling water spray all over the blanket. The second morning, when my alarm woke me, my tea appeared to have been brewed about 3am and was stone cold. On the third morning I threw the machine into the bin.

The heady scent of city life also failed to live up to my expectations. I clearly had no idea of what traffic on

Celebrating my 21st birthday in Brighton, 1960, where The King Brothers were appearing in a summer season with Frankie Vaughan, Tommy Cooper, Roy Castle, and some very tasty young ladies (apart from the one on the left with the big hooter).

the Fulham Road would be like or I would never have deliberately chosen a second-floor front flat, especially as I was the first tenant in a new block that backed onto a quiet mews and could have had my pick. Life was marginally less noisy in the winter than the summer, when you had to keep the windows open or die of heatstroke, although with them open, black clouds of exhaust from the heavy lorries billowed in. It must have occurred to me to move, but I didn't. I stuck it out for five years, paying £400 per year in rent, which worked out to just over £7 a week. (Actor friend Julian Holloway paid slightly less for his flat around the corner in Sloane Avenue Mansions – but then, of course, he didn't have the view.)

As far as my dream of girls tripping over each other to spend the night with me in my swinging state-of-the-art bachelor pad, Miranda the ex-Bluebell from the Pheasantry Club I'd won through table tennis skills, while by no means a one-off, never exactly triggered the stampede I'd been expecting. ("Come in, my dear, come in! Forgive the earplugs and gas mask. Sorry about the traffic. May I offer you a drink?")

The journey from 216 Fulham Road to Shaftesbury Avenue in my pale blue MGB took 11 minutes and to me, and a lot of others, Shaftesbury Avenue did not mean "the theatre". It meant Gerry's.

Gerry's Club, between Frith and Dean Streets, was *the* place to go. It was founded, named after, and run by a lovable character named Gerry Campion, a little round man with a high-pitched voice and a quick temper and who was principally known for portraying Billy Bunter on television. The food was cheap and cheerful, the drinks reasonably priced, and the place attracted everyone from out-of-and-in-work actors, to writers, producers, casting agents, musicians, showgirls and the occasional Hollywood movie star. We all ended up at Gerry's. One of the legendary regulars – and drinkers – was actor, writer, and lyricist John Junkin.

John and I had known one another since 1961 and had developed not only a firm friendship but a writing partnership which produced songs for Matt Monro, Marty Feldman and probably more than 200 deeply satisfying collaborations for the BBC radio comedy series *Hello Cheeky* – classic songs, such as *District Nurse Hargreaves*, *Moon Over Romford* and *Those Yellow Lights On The Bayswater Road Made You Look Chinese To Me*. After a fruitful afternoon song-writing at my bachelor pad, we would head to Gerry's on Shaftesbury Avenue (where I parked my car right outside, no yellow lines in those days) install ourselves at a table and, assisted by scotch or lager (me), Guinness, vodka, brandy and port and anything else (John), lose all track of time joke telling and laughing ourselves senseless with whomever came in and invariably be kicked out by Gerry at midnight. We did this night after night when I wasn't performing. Despite the vast amounts of alcohol I must have consumed, only very rarely did I ever feel, look or act intoxicated. John was another story.

An extremely gifted and intelligent man, he was frighteningly quick-witted (he was the principal creator, along with Tim Brooke-Taylor, of the nonsense game *Mornington Crescent*, which was born at Gerry's Club). John could be sparkling company, unless he'd had much too much to drink, at which point he could – not always but often – become morose or bitter or given to aggressive outbursts of all three. I fell foul of him only once, having stolen his date when he went to the loo, something I'm not particularly proud of but it was a bit of a coup at the time as his date happened to be Groucho Marx's daughter and rather attractive (apart from the moustache and cigar). It's the only time I can think of, however, when his fury was justified. Far more career-damaging was his reaction to the then BBC Head of Light Entertainment, the amiable Bill Cotton Jr.

John and Tim Brooke-Taylor had written and appeared in a comedy series for the BBC called *The Rough With The Smooth*. As I understand it, the Beeb, having promised them a peak-time slot for transmission, kept messing them about, changing schedules, saying one thing and doing the other, and both John and Tim were becoming increasingly frustrated and annoyed. Early one evening, in a sparsely populated Gerry's, I was sitting at the bar with an especially grumpy John when down the stairs bounded Bill Cotton.

"Hello, John!" Bill said, brightly.

John glanced up. "Hello, c**t!" he growled, thus swiftly ending his relationship with the BBC for ever (and never quite understanding why).

Persuading John to call it a night was like telling a bomb to stop ticking. The only thing that would have prevented him buying another round or a bottle of champagne just when you were getting your coats on would have been sudden death. We were still drinking, late one night, when in came two showgirls from The Talk of The Town, a nightclub on the corner of Leicester Square. John knew one of them slightly and they joined us for a drink (his seventh vodka) after which Gerry wanted to close and booted us out. I was ready to go home (would I have driven my car? I'm ashamed to say I think I would have), but John insisted we all go on somewhere. The girls were keen, so off we went and "somewhere" ended up being The Stork Club, a well-known clip joint in nearby Swallow Street, Mayfair.

When we entered the dimly-lit club, a tatty cabaret was just finishing. We were shown to a table. There seemed to be only a couple of others occupied. Through the gloom I could see a drunken Tony Hancock with a small group, and there was a larger, noisier one at the far end of the room. We ordered over-priced and probably watered-down drinks and listened to John tell jokes (however plastered he got he never forgot a punchline). A four-piece band of bored-looking musicians struck up. Out of the corner of my eye, I noticed Hancock and his party stagger out. Suddenly, beside our table, loomed a large male figure, looking uncomfortably like one of Ronnie Corbett's old camel-hair-coated admirers from Swiss Cottage.

"Oi, darlin'," he said to my date, Jackie, interrupting our conversation. "Come on, 'ave a dance wiv me."

I tensed. Jackie politely explained that she was with someone. Camel Hair muttered something and went away. Moments later, another figure appeared at my shoulder, this time a large blowsy blonde.

"Who d'ya fink you are, you fuckin' bitch?" she cried, before striking Jackie in the face with her handbag and drawing blood. "You wouldn't dance wiv my old man?"

"Hey!" I said, pulling myself up to my full imposing five foot five and three-quarter inches, a King Brother to the rescue, but before I could figure out what to do, a hand grabbed my shoulder, spun me round, punched me in the mouth, and I went flying across the table, spitting teeth. My natural reaction – unbelievably – was to retaliate, but Junkin, all six foot two of him by this time under the table quaking with fear, grabbed my foot and, pulling me down, yelled "Forget it, Den! There's more of them!", and indeed, the last image I had before being yanked under the tablecloth was of an army of camel-haired gorillas bearing down on us from across the room.

(Sadly, for a hero, I have no recollection whatsoever as to what the girls were doing during all this.)

Then, like the cavalry coming over the hill, eight or 10 waiters materialised and somehow managed to intercept and bundle the villains out the front door, whereupon, full of blood lust, they beat up two passing Indian tourists, we found out later, leaving them senseless in the gutter.

When John and I surfaced, the manager of the Stork Club apologised but said he had no idea who the heavies were and denied any liability (and didn't even offer us a complimentary drink, which pissed Junkin off). After thanking John rather sarcastically and lispingly for a hugely entertaining evening, I spent a restless night alone on my divan bed in my bachelor pad wondering how I was going to appear at the Palladium without my front teeth and how I could bring thothe bathtardths to juthtith.

At about four in the morning, I suddenly remembered The King Brothers had done a couple of charity shows for Scotland Yard and had befriended a Superintendent Dagg of the Flying Squad. My plan, which I worked on until it was time to get up, was to get in touch with this Dagg, tell him the story, he'd take charge, the camel-hairs would be rounded up and brought to trial, found guilty, taken through the streets of London in a tumbrel to Gerry's, where, before a cheering crowd of club regulars, they would be slowly disembowelled with a rusty Swiss Army knife, but before I had a chance to contact Dagg of the Yard or even find his number, my phone rang. It was Jackie, my date from the night before.

"I'd better warn you," she said. "Don't even think of contacting the police."

"Oh?" I said, disappointed. "Why not?"

Jackie explained that her boyfriend was a croupier and occasionally mixed in unsavoury circles. Having heard the details of the night before, he'd said "Tell your friend to forget it!"

She went on to say the Stork Club paid regular protection money to the Richardson Gang, well-known South London gangsters who made the Kray twins seem like choirboys. Also known as "The Torture Gang", their speciality was pinning victims to the floor with six inch nails and removing their toes with bolt cutters. It seemed the Stork Club had been late with its payments so the heavies had been sent in to cause trouble. If I so much as breathed a word to the police, there would be a knock on my door, guaranteed.

Suddenly the idea of playing the Palladium with no teeth seemed an absolute doddle compared to performing with my hands nailed to the Steinway, and so instead of Scotland Yard I rang the dentist. He fixed me up. My new teeth lasted 25 years, thanks to Mr. Barry Bloom at 19a Cavendish Square, the Richardson Gang eventually ended up in I believe, Wormwood Scrubs (nothing to do with me, honest!) and I learned a valuable lesson: never, ever leave Gerry's Club, ever. Especially with John Junkin.

Chapter 11

FRANK, TONY, NINA, AND ROY

Frank Sinatra was and always will be my favourite singer of all time. Harold Davidson, an agent-impresario whom The King Brothers knew from doing a TV series for Granada called *Swing Along* with Des O'Connor and Marion Ryan (Harold's girlfriend), was putting together a midnight charity show at the Royal Festival Hall starring Sinatra, and asked if we'd like to appear on the show. The date clashed with a possible gig with the Dagenham Girl Pipers at the Lawn's Way Social Club in Romford but, strangely enough, we opted to go with Frank.

Harold was then Sinatra's European representative. He promised us that Frank would watch our act, be suitably impressed, and no doubt within weeks we'd be boarding his private jet direct to the Sands Hotel in Las Vegas. The thought of not only meeting but working with my hero was all-consuming and I counted the days to the concert.

Sinatra didn't show at the afternoon rehearsal. His band did, and the disappointment at not chewing the fat with Frank over a cup of tea was marginally tempered by getting to hear those marvellous musicians at close quarters. By show time Frank still hadn't appeared. I'd been hanging around the stage door in my dress suit since 10pm waiting for him. Around 11pm there was a sudden hullabaloo when a figure in a white trench coat and snap brim hat came in, accompanied by shrieks and girlish screams from outside, and I thought it was My Man but it turned out to be Johnny Dankworth, who looked not unlike him, and who was leading his own orchestra which opened the show.

At midnight, before a glittering audience full of stars and royals, the performance got underway. Still no sign of F.S. I was getting anxious. The King Brothers were on soon, he was going to miss us!

When we did finally go on, I spent most of our opening number, *Hey! Look Me Over!* glancing into the wings, fully expecting to see Frank standing there beaming and giving us the thumbs up.

No sign.

We did two more numbers, finishing with *Yes, Indeed!*, a song for which we had had a clever, but extremely complicated (for us), dance routine devised by Sammy Davis' choreographer, Alex Plaschette. The idea was we'd play and sing the first verse, then let the Dankworth band take over, abandon our instruments and get up and dance, but for some reason Dankworth set the dance tempo twice as fast as we'd rehearsed it and we ended up racing around the stage like Cossacks, practically with sparks coming from our shoes trying to fit in all the steps, and eventually exiting Stage Right in a puff of smoke. Heart pounding, gasping for breath, I hurriedly got changed and returned to my vigil by the stage door as the interval began. Almost immediately, the stage door flew open. Five or six large men in suits burst in and in the centre of them, wearing Johnny Dankworth's outfit, was the man himself. In the flesh. "What the hell time do you

Midnight, Friday, June 1st, 1962

at the

PROGRAMME

Royal Festival Hall
London

JOHNNY DANKWORTH
AND HIS ORCHESTRA

NORMAN VAUGHAN

THE KING BROTHERS

CLEO LAINE

INTERMISSION

DAVID JACOBS
INTRODUCES

FRANK SINATRA

ACCOMPANIED BY THE
BILL MILLER SEXTET

Programme for the Royal Festival Hall, 1962. A midnight charity concert in which The King Brothers appeared with my all-time hero, Francis Albert. (Well, we weren't on stage at the same time, exactly.)

call *this*, Francis Albert, you missed our act!" I thought, but just stood there, gawking, with a big silly grin. Sinatra was hustled straight past and into his dressing room. Two of the large besuited men remained outside as sentries.

The second act began with emcee David Jacobs introducing Sinatra's band. I now positioned myself in the wings where I had an unobstructed view of both the stage and Frank's dressing room door. I was going to miss nothing. As the band struck up the intro to *Goody Goody*, the dressing room door opened. My pulse rate quickened.

With perfect timing, an immaculately-attired Ol' Blue Eyes strode out and went directly onstage, to thunderous applause – but not before a curt nod in my direction. At least I think it was to me, there was no one behind me. (And it wasn't unfriendly. Curt, perhaps, but meaningful.)

This was 1962 and Sinatra was at the peak of his powers. The voice was from another planet, a gift from the gods. I was transfixed. Seventy-five minutes flew by. As he finished his final encore, the band still playing, the audience now on their feet going wild – Frank Sinatra came offstage, nodded again to me, but this time added an equally curt, but meaningful "Hi, kid!" before heading out the door into his waiting limo. As I watched it drive off, I had a vision of Frank being already back in his suite at the Savoy in bed with a couple of blondes and a Jack Daniels on the rocks by the time the band had finished *Come Fly With Me*. Perhaps he was.

The King Brothers, curiously, were not invited to the Sands in Las Vegas.

I had a slightly longer conversation with another hero of mine, the singer Tony Bennett. In 1955 I used to walk along the promenade on my way to the Central Pier Theatre in Morecambe every day and the music spilling from an amusement arcade always seemed to be *Stranger In Paradise*. That's when I first heard the name Tony Bennett. What a voice, I thought! Electrifying. Distinctive. Some people may be surprised to hear me speak of Bennett and Sinatra in the same breath but for me, although Tony Bennett may not have Sinatra's technical brilliance, he has a joyous quality, a love of life, and therefore an emotional power which never fails to move me. He's also a wonderful musician and his voice was one of the few things that put a smile on my face that whole summer season.

Seven years later I went to New York for the first time when the wonderful entertainer – and friend – Roy Castle was doing a TV series over there. Bennett was then riding high in the US charts with *I Left My Heart In San Francisco*, which seemed to be on the radio every few minutes. Once again I was captivated by the voice. Three years after that, back in London, I got a call from Roy. He'd been invited by Tony Bennett to come for tea at his hotel.

"You *know* Tony Bennett?" I said, impressed.

"Yes. I just did a show with him in the States. Want to come and meet him?"

When we knocked at the door to Bennett's suite at the Mayfair, the familiar, laid-back and slightly husky voice called out "Come on in, Roy!" We pushed open the door. Tony Bennett, his face covered in shaving foam, stuck his head out of the bathroom door and waved.

"Hi!" he smiled. Roy introduced me as a musician friend. "You play piano?" Bennett asked. I said that I did.

"Great! Play something for me."

With his razor, he indicated a white baby grand in the

corner of the room, then stepped back into the bathroom, door open, and continued shaving. I asked what he'd like me to play.

"Do you know *Here's That Rainy Day*? In G?"

I said I did.

"Hey great! Play it for me!"

I sat down at the piano. As I started to play, Tony Bennett started to sing, I assume while still shaving.

MAYBE, I SHOULD HAVE SAVED
THOSE LEFTOVER DREAMS,
FUNNY, BUT HERE'S THAT RAINY DAY...

There it was, that voice! But coming from the bathroom instead of the radio! We went through the entire song. I could barely see straight. Me! Accompanying Tony Bennett! Shaving! Roy watched it all with a smile, rather like a proud father.

We had tea, Bennett was charming, I can't remember anything else, I probably went home and for the next month told everyone I knew I'd met Tony Bennett. I didn't see him again until our mutual friend Benny Green's funeral 30 years later, a less joyous occasion, and no one much felt like singing.

Meeting someone you've admired from afar is always a thrill – well, perhaps not always, but if that someone turns out to be nice as well as talented, you admire them even more, and if you manage to enter their world, however briefly, and be accepted, the thrill is magnified to the extent that you won't hear a bad word against them, ever.

The actress Georgia Brown gave a party at her house in Knightsbridge one night. I think Albert Finney was the one who'd actually been invited and actor Julian Holloway and I were just tagging along. There was a six-foot Steinway grand in the room (I may be hopelessly unobservant in matters of décor or, say, my wife's wardrobe, but I never forget a piano) and unable to ignore the magnetic force that draws me ever closer to a keyboard when I see one, especially a very nice one, I found myself, at some stage during the evening, running my hands over the ebony finish.

"Darling, do play something!" the hostess pleaded, which was wholly unnecessary as I was already seated, fingers poised. In these situations, unless someone wishes to do a special party piece, I'm quite happy to go into "cocktail pianist mode", meaning not playing anything too intrusive or too loud and keeping very much in the background. I was happily tinkling a bit of Gershwin when I sensed a commotion by the front door. I looked up and saw Nina Simone. Nina Simone the blues singer, Nina Simone the jazz pianist, Nina Simone the legend I'd always admired from afar – precisely the place from which to admire her too, I'd heard, as she had a reputation for being troublesome, moody and not the easiest of company.

Nina surveyed the room, zeroed in on the Steinway, then me, then headed over with a fierce expression on her face and sat herself down next to me on the piano stool, fortunately a large one.

"Hey." She gave me a nudge. "Let's play something together."

"Oh!" I said, trying not to sound relieved. "Of course. What would you like to…"

"Twelve-bar blues. B flat. I take the top, you take the bass."

A twelve-bar blues, for those of you who don't know,

is a chord sequence of twelve bars based on a traditional set pattern, and originated in the early part of the last century in America's Deep South. It's basically just a chord sequence, and one which has lent itself to work songs, jazz, rock and roll, and country. In a blues song this twelve bar progression is repeated over and over through the course of the tune. Players improvise within the specific musical parameters. It can be played in any key but uses the same basic sequence of chords.

I started an intro. Nina adjusted her bracelets, then joined in. We played a couple of choruses. I gradually realised the room had gone quiet: the entire party was focused on Nina and me (I wish somebody had taken a picture). We played on. It seemed to be going well. Nina turned to me and smiled. I smiled back.

"Hey, man." She gave me an affectionate squeeze. "You swing!"

I think, I *hope* I managed to say "Thanks!" but I'm not sure, because I tell you, for a little white Catholic short-arse from Hornchurch to be told by a big black American jazz legend that you swing – well, it doesn't get much better than that.

At approximately 8.45pm one Sunday night, back on stage at the London Palladium, live, in front of not just the 2,300 faces in the theatre but a television audience of 18 million, I experienced a sudden awareness of how I would look if I screwed up, and how I would look, I realised, was like a complete pillock. I panicked.

This had never happened before. It wasn't an oh-dear-God-I-think-I-may-have-to-kill-myself type panic, but it was enough to put a damper on whatever enjoyment I had previously found in performing and, with very few exceptions, the looming shadow of Performing Pillock

Man has stayed with me to this day.

No one noticed it, that evening on *Sunday Night at the London Palladium*, not even my brothers. My smile might have seemed a bit forced if you inspected it closely, but I played and sang as normal. A few months later, though, on *The Roy Castle Show*, Performing Pillock Man did finally make his live television debut.

Charming, modest, incredibly talented, Roy Castle could do anything. He danced, he sang, told jokes, played trumpet, drums (and golf). We'd done countless shows together, shared houses and summer seasons; he'd become a close friend of the entire King clan. My brothers and I had appeared on his television show many times, but on this particular occasion I had been given a line to say in a sketch of Roy's that would follow our act. Not since my triumph in short trousers at the Casino Theatre, Southport, playing an urchin buying flowers for his blind mother had I been asked to dazzle audiences with my acting ability and, although slightly nervous, I sailed through rehearsals and my confidence grew.

Minutes before the live transmission, the writers, Sid Green and Dick Hills, came into our dressing room and said to me: "We want to change your line." It wasn't a big change, they said, only a slight re-jigging of the words to make it funnier. I begged them not to. I'd been practising my line all week and was getting rather good at it. They laughed and went out, not noticing my transformation into Performing Pillock Man. I looked down at my new line change as, over the Tannoy, the floor manager called The King Brothers to the set.

According to the script, after we had performed *Mais Oui* and *Buona Sera*, Roy Castle would come on carrying a cardboard box, out of which he would pull a folded shirt and say something like "Hey, fellas, what do you think of my new shirt? It's a drip-dry!"

And I would say something like "Oh? I didn't know you could get drip-dry shirts in a box!", after which Roy supplied the big punchline, whatever that might have been. I'd be more specific, but I must have blocked it all.

The red light came on, the cameras rolled, we sang our two numbers with our usual cheery demeanour, during which I thought of nothing but drip-dry shirts and boxes and becoming more and more muddled as to what my line was or had been or wasn't any more. Roy entered on cue after our applause, with his box. He gave me his line, then looked at me expectantly. The camera moved in for a close-up. I stared at Roy, wild-eyed. Puzzled, and with a half smile, he inclined his head, waiting. We'd never rehearsed the new line, possibly he thought I was coming up with something even funnier. My mouth opened. Nothing came out. Still he waited. Sweat ran down my back.

"I'm – sorry!" I blurted, heart pounding, and then to his astonishment ran right past him, and his drip-dry shirt, off the set (and possibly out of the building). The whole experience was horrific, humiliating, and mortifying. It still is, even reliving it now. Poor Roy. To his credit, he was awfully nice about it. But then, he was an awfully nice man.

Chapter 12

HABERDASHERY, HEART TRANSPLANTS, AND A JIMI HENDRIX EXPERIENCE

By 1967, work for "Britain's Youngest Rhythm Aces" was becoming distinctly hard to come by. The safe, clean-cut family entertainment that had seen us through our career had given way to a new form of popular music. Variety was dead, tastes had changed. Basically, the music scene had changed and we hadn't. Well, apart from growing older. Travelling around the country to smoke-filled Working Men's Clubs to perform between the wrestling and the stripper was more or less all the work we could find. The trouble was, it's all we knew. Growing up a King Brother doesn't prepare you for much else besides being a King Brother.

Over the years, between gigs, Mike once worked at a place called Briggs Motor Bodies, and Tony had briefly tried being a clerk in a building company. My only attempt at a "proper job" had been at the age of 17 when I became what was called an "extrusionist" at a company called Lacrinoids, a terrifying job which involved feeding waste plastic into a giant cutter with no safety guard. I was convinced I was going to fall in or at the very least lose a hand. I lasted one day. Tony and I at one point even made a pathetic foray into menswear, despite the fact that neither of us knew the difference between cash flow and cashmere and, in truth, hardly ever went clothes shopping.

Whether we were beginning to have nagging thoughts about life post-King Brothers, or just hoping to cash in on the Carnaby Street band wagon, or a little of both, or perhaps because we were just plain foolish, I'm not certain, but Tony and I were persuaded by Barry Knight, then a cricketing all-rounder for Essex and England whom I knew from charity cricket matches, to invest in a new menswear boutique in Mayfair – to be named, most seductively, The House of Kings. We were talked into investing £2,000 each (about £12,000 in total, today).

Barry and his business partner, Bernie Segal, set the whole thing up. They found the premises, kitted it out, chose the merchandise, and the The House of Kings had a grand showbiz opening with much fanfare, champagne, press, stars, the works. Harry Secombe headed the celebrity list. Tony and I buzzed around raising our glasses right and left, congratulating ourselves on our brilliant business acumen, assuming the heaving crowds fighting to get in would be a daily occurrence.

The morning after the grand opening The King Brothers went away on tour. Upon our return, two weeks later, Tony and I raced over to Avery Row behind Bond Street to visit our thriving enterprise and were surprised to see a sign in the window that said "SALE NOW ON!". The only one in the shop was a surly, spotty youth, who also appeared to be in charge.

"Wot d'you want?" he said, chewing a sandwich.

"We're the owners," we said. "This is our shop. We're The Kings! Where's Barry?"

"'E's gorn orf. To Barbados, wiv Bernie. Oh, and two young ladies."

We asked why there was a sale on, barely two weeks after we'd opened. The youth said we hadn't shifted any stock and owed a couple of suppliers already.

"But, how could this happen?" we asked, horrified.

"Dunno," the youth said, picking cucumber out of his teeth.

Tony and I left the shop and made our respective ways home with long faces, a cut-price shirt and a pair of socks each. Some weeks later we were called to a creditors' meeting. The House of Kings was being sued, we were told, and the company filing for bankruptcy. Barry said to us: "Sorry guys, it just didn't work out!", promptly moved to Australia, and when last heard of was coaching cricketers in Sydney.

Out of the blue, The King Brothers were invited to appear on Simon Dee's *Dee Time*, a popular weekly live entertainment TV show from Manchester, a job we were more than happy to slot in between appearances at Greasbrough Working Men's Club and Leigh Miners Welfare Institute Recreation and Social Centre. We piled into our newly-acquired second-hand Chevrolet Impala station wagon (our first non-Ford, much to Dad's disgust) and drove to the studio, parked, unloaded, had a cup of tea, did the camera rehearsal, and were still in our sharp matching sweaters and bow ties when the door opened and in came the act with whom we were sharing our dressing room – a tall black man in platform shoes with a mass of frizzy hair, followed by two smallish white guys, all of them dressed in grubby, creased and sweat-stained satin shirts. They'd just done a gig in Scotland, explained the one carrying in a crate of Guinness, had slept in the van, and here they were. The tall guy smiled.

"Hi there. I'm Jimi Hendrix," he said, and offered us a toke from an enormous spliff. We introduced ourselves, shook hands, but declined the spliff. Tony politely shared a Guinness.

Within the year, Hendrix, whom no one had then heard of, including us, was one of the biggest rock stars in the world (his commemorative blue plaque, curiously, is next to Handel's on Brook Street in Mayfair). The King Brothers, meanwhile, not to be outdone, were busy distinguishing themselves as The Merry Men in a Christmas pantomime up in Derby (Tony claims it was Southampton, maybe it was) where Robin Hood was played by a 60-year-old singer called Donald Peers who had once been famous for his hit *In A Shady Nook By A Babbling Brook*, and Maid Marian was played by an 18-year-old New Zealand girl who was a foot taller than he was. I'm being charitable when I say that it was the cheapest, tattiest production I have ever seen let alone been in.

The three King Brothers, dressed in threadbare Lincoln Green doublets and baggy hose, were the full extent of Robin's band of Merry Men. Having "discovered" a clearing in the "forest" (two cardboard trees) in which a piano, a bass and a guitar had been conveniently "abandoned", we performed two songs which had literally nothing to do with Robin Hood. I was furthermore required to play "The Ghost", which necessitated a fast change in the wings into a dirty white bed sheet with two holes snipped out for eyes and a rubber band around my neck, whereupon I would race back onstage just in time to "scare" the two Babes in the Wood. If you were lucky, one of the few kids still in the audience would yell "He's behind you!" but if not, the stage manager, from the wings, in a high voice, would. The panto lasted a remarkable two weeks and is chiefly remembered in the annals of King Brother history for some thought-provoking philosophical advice bestowed upon us backstage by an Irish comedy double act playing the Robbers, Syd and Max Harrison: "Don't dig your grave with your penis!"

When Nat Berlin, a booking agent, rang with an offer of three weeks in sunny Cape Town and Johannesburg working with a well-known American comedian, Myron Cohen, then a big star in South Africa, we grabbed it. We hoped audiences there would like us, obviously, but were unprepared for the reception we got: they loved us! I can only put this down to the fact that in 1967 television had yet to reach South Africa and we arrived there as complete unknowns, the result being that everything we did seemed fresh and new. Mr. Percy Baneshik, Johannesburg theatre critic, called us "the sonic boom of the show", Mr. Bill Edgson generously wrote that our selection of material was excellent and he "could have listened to us for hours" and Mr. Terry Herbst of *The Cape Times* had this report:

"The King Brothers, three small but talented Englishmen, drew a tremendous and seldom heard response from a first-night audience. Neat and clean-looking, they showed a superlative precision style and fully deserved the rousing ovation they got."

I'm not sure I personally would have dropped everything to run and see us, based on that review, but South Africans certainly did, and, having been used to our audiences in Working Men's Clubs getting up to dance or go to the loo when we came on, it was not only a novelty but a decidedly pleasurable experience seeing people on their feet, whooping and clapping along to *If I Were A Rich Man* and calling for encores.

Up until committing this incident to paper, it had been my clear recollection that Dr. Christiaan Barnard, the famous heart surgeon, came backstage one night after the show in Cape Town and we were all introduced. The event had been accompanied by heavy press coverage, especially because Barnard had brought along with him his celebrated patient, Louis Washkansky, the world's first human heart transplant recipient, a frail-looking gentleman in a tartan dressing gown who was being constantly fussed over by a team of nurses.

When I fondly related the incident to my wife, however, in the process of writing this book, she asked, not unreasonably perhaps, why in the world Washkansky would be taken out of intensive care to go to the theatre (to see The King Brothers) when the man had only had the transplant operation a few days before (and in fact died a few days later). She had a point.

Somewhat unsettled, I went on the internet to find documentation of this momentous meet – articles, headlines, photos of us all grouped happy and smiling around the wheelchair, arms round one another, taking Washkansky's pulse, adjusting his drip line, anything. But there was nothing, not a scrap. Confused, I rang Mike and Tony. They don't even remember meeting Christaan Barnard, let alone Louis Washkansky.

My wife then noticed that the glowing review of the

small, but talented King Brothers, in *The Cape Times* was dated not 1967 but 1968, which prompted further discussion, and has resulted in the worrying conclusion that I couldn't possibly have met Louis Washkansky backstage or anywhere else because the poor man had been dead for a year.

The realisation that I've spent more than 40 years relating a vivid encounter that never happened is not only devastating but has, in fact, warranted the pouring of a large Glenfiddich on the rocks several hours earlier than normal.

Chapter 13

THE TUPPERWARE BRIGADE

To appear at the Albert Hall in front of an audience of 5,000 screaming women might well be a normal everyday occurrence for the likes of Rod Stewart or Robbie Williams, but for us it was a first. Regrettably, however, the audience response was not due to a sudden attack of King Brother Fever sweeping the country. It was, I hesitate to say this, a Tupperware convention.

I haven't the faintest idea why our act was chosen, or what our connection with plastic storage boxes might have been, but we didn't question it. It was, after all, a job. We performed at approximately 10.30 in the morning, just after the delegates had had their coffee and biscuits and just before the winning salesladies, accompanied by a renewed surge of mass hysteria, were presented with their awards.

We sang *There's No Business Like Show Business*, *High Society* and one with which you may be less familiar, *The Tupperware Brigade.*

Some weeks earlier, the organisers of the event had approached me to write an original song, a sort of Tupperware anthem celebrating their Fifth Distributors Conference, a recording of which would be handed out to the 5,000 Tupperware conventionees as a souvenir of the day. Thus inspired, I came up with a tune, to which writer friend John Junkin set a similarly inspiring lyric. The King Brothers, along with drummer Martin Aston, recorded it on the Tupperware Label (I kid you not) at Abbey Road Studios. It had been our first time back there since Parlophone had cancelled our contract five years earlier.

The recording went swimmingly.

Afterwards, a musician friend from another session was in the process of putting his gear into the boot of his car when he witnessed the following exchange on the front steps of the studios:

As my brother Tony was coming out, carrying his double bass, he was stopped by a young man with a guitar case, bounding up the steps, coming in. The young man stopped.

"Tony! Hi! How are you?" he said with a big smile.

Tony returned the smile but with some hesitation. "Er, fine thanks."

"You don't remember me, do you?" the young man said.

"You look familiar." Tony admitted, clearly trying to place him. "Have we met?"

"We came to see you at the Liverpool Empire. You and your brothers. About five or six years ago. We got your autographs. And you came to a party with us after the show on the Saturday night."

Tony still looked puzzled.

"It's Paul. Paul McCartney."

"Ohhh – yes," said Tony, after a beat. "That's right. Well, nice to see you."

"What are you doing here, then?" McCartney asked.

At this point, Tony's face lit up. "We've just recorded *The Tupperware Brigade*," he said rather proudly. "What about you?"

"We're making a new album," said McCartney.

"Oh? Well done." Tony nodded politely. "What's it called?"

"*Sergeant Pepper's Lonely Hearts Club Band.*"

Tony nodded politely again. "Well – good luck with it! Nice to see you," he added and continued down the steps, bass on his back, to the car.

This was 1967. The Beatles were everywhere. The music of John, Paul, George and Ringo had taken over the world. Despite my dad being incensed by their very existence and when seeing them on TV would refer to them as "those bloody long-haired bastards", their four famous faces were, without question, the most recognisable on earth. Except of course to Tony King who, I should explain, lest you think Mike and I are saddled with a halfwit for a brother, has a rather endearing tendency at times to reside on another planet, to the extent that neither Mike nor I were remotely surprised by the McCartney story.

Unlike *With A Little Help From My Friends* or indeed any of the tracks on the *Sergeant Pepper* album, *The Tupperware Brigade* has not, to my knowledge, been recorded by any other artists, but surely deserves its own place in popular music history. I would like to suggest that that place be in a time capsule buried under the Albert Hall, carefully preserved in a one-litre Tupperware Space-Saver Bowl, but I'll let you be the judge:

129

WHO'S THE HAPPIEST HOUSEWIFE
IN THE KITCHEN
THE ONE WITH TUPPERWARE ON THE SHELF?
I TELL YOU ANY HOUSEWIFE FINDS THAT IT'S
BEWITCHIN',
IT'S LIGHT, IT'S BRIGHT,
THE PRICE IS RIGHT AND YOU CAN MAKE
SOME CASH YOURSELF
WE'RE GIVING A PARTY SOON AND YOU CAN
COME FOR FREE
SO COME ALONG AND SEE,
WE'RE SURE THAT YOU'LL AGREE

Chorus:

TUPPERWARE! TUPPERWARE!
IS THE FINEST KITCHEN WARE
THAT WAS EVER MADE,
TUPPERWARE! TUPPERWARE!
FALL IN AND JOIN
THE TUPPERWARE BRIGADE!

THEY'VE GOT A RANGE OF KITCHEN GOODS
THAT ARE THE BEST
WHY DON'T YOU COME ALONG
AND PUT THEM TO THE TEST?
ONCE YOU'VE TRIED THEM
YOU'LL AGREE IT'S TRUE,
ALL THE THINGS THAT WE ARE TELLING YOU!

Then repeat the chorus (until the whole world is singing).

There must surely come a point in everyone's life where

one looks around and says to oneself: "What am I doing here?", and in my case this moment occurred when opening a piano lid in a leaky barn in a remote field somewhere outside Clonmel in southern Ireland to see if I could discover why some of the notes were sticking. Imagine one of those magician's cylinders out of which an enormous bouquet of flowers explodes. Piano wires sprung out at me, pinging in all directions. This piano, looking not unlike it had been previously bounced down a flight of steps by Laurel and Hardy, was the instrument I was expected to play an hour later. The King Brothers were halfway through a 10-day tour of one-night stands put together by a shadowy Irish promoter named Seamus Bohan who, needless to say, was nowhere to be seen.

Nor, in fact, was an audience. Up until about 15 minutes before the "curtain", if you can call it that, there had been no signs of life in or around the barn other than us, a drunken caretaker-stage manager, and his cat. We were convinced we'd got the day wrong or were in the wrong barn. Then, suddenly, swarming towards us over the hill like a scene from the film *Zulu*, came our audience – in cars, trucks, bikes, old carts, and the odd horse. Within seconds the barn was packed to capacity.

We performed as best as we could, me on the broken down upright, which continued to disintegrate throughout the act. Surprisingly, the audience appeared to have a good time. Maybe they didn't get out much. Our big finish was to be our former hit *Standing On The Corner*. People always expected it. We had decided earlier, roughly about the time I ducked to avoid being decapitated by a rogue zinging piano wire, that as a safeguard we would *mime* to our recording of the song.

We gave our 45rpm record to the caretaker-stage

manager and instructed him to play it at the appropriate
time over the sound system. Miraculously, he did. On it
came, right on cue, loud and clear – but unfortunately at the
frenetic speed of 78rpm, not 45rpm, and so, much to the
audience's bafflement, *Standing On The Corner* was
performed, start to finish, by Alvin and the Chipmunks.

The question "What am I doing here?" was by now
something I was asking myself approximately every seven
seconds and after discovering that not only had Seamus
Bohan bounced our pay cheque but bounced the one to the
Gresham Hotel, Dublin, as well, leaving us to pay for our
10-day stay or be sued, there was no doubt in my mind,
by the completion of the tour, that the end of The King
Brothers was nigh.

After a joyless, dismal stint at the Playboy Club back
in London playing to six Arabs and a Bunny, I decided
I'd had enough. I think we all had. Mike, Tony and I
had a meeting, and the matching blazers with the KBs on
the pockets that our mum had lovingly sewn on, were
consigned to the attic. Not counting the Manchester
United Munich air disaster in 1958, the disbanding of The
King Brothers was genuinely the saddest day of Dad's
life, and from then on he wasn't much interested in
anything any of us ever did.

The year was 1970.

William Anthony King (Tony) had been married for
some six years to a pretty, Leslie Roberts Silhouettes
dancer he'd met in Blackpool, Candy Scott, and with
whom he has recently celebrated his 50th wedding
anniversary. They have three children and five
grandchildren. After the act broke up Tony went to work
for a music publisher, then became a plumber, a
milkman, an insurance salesman, and then a bank clerk
for Lloyds until he was made redundant, whereupon to

alleviate boredom he took up tap dancing, yoga and French lessons while working as a bagger in Safeways. He's now retired, plays golf and, according to his wife, falls asleep in front of the TV a lot. When I began compiling notes for these memoirs, I sent both brothers a list of questions, one of which was "Were you happy being a King Brother?" and to Mike's and my absolute astonishment, because Tony never acted remotely stage-struck and we'd always thought of him as dependably unexcitable, ambling rather placidly along whatever happened, good or bad – Tony answered, without hesitation, that he'd "loved performing" and that "the thrill of playing to packed houses was second to none!".

Mike married actress Carol White (of the ground-breaking TV docu-drama *Cathy Come Home* fame) in 1962, and was in the process of divorce when our act disbanded. He has two sons and one grandchild and has never remarried. Because his handwriting is notoriously indecipherable, he answered my questions verbally into a tape recorder, but not numbered or in any discernible order, the result being I can't find a particular answer when I need it (or indeed even the tape recorder itself now) but I feel safe in saying that performing as a King Brother was, for Michael John King, inarguably the highpoint of his life. He loved the attention, he loved the limelight. I think it is also safe to say that no job since has ever fulfilled him in the same way, or indeed in any way. Lying on a bed reading a library book and swimming in the Hampstead Heath Ponds does seem to have the greatest appeal, although over the years Mike has managed to work briefly for EMI Records, Thames TV, producer Danny O'Donovan, others who escape me, and he once founded a short-lived film production company named Tinseltown with actor Robert Powell and Sheik

Abdulla Al Khalifa of Bahrain. Notable experiences include being fired by director Michael Winner in a hotel in New York City for being one minute late with a wake-up call, and going on Robert Powell's honeymoon with him to Franco Zeffirelli's villa in Positano when Babs Lord, Robert's lovely new wife, couldn't make it at the last minute due to a *Top Of The Pops* gig with her dance troupe, Pan's People. Mike has also flown in Pia Zadora's private jet and once met Salman Rushdie and Claus Von Bulow in the same evening.

By 1970 I had already been briefly engaged to one (or perhaps it was the other) of the Baker Twins, Susan and Jennifer, identical singing dancing pretty blondes, but was by now a year into my marriage to Caryl Arrol, the young widow of comedian Don Arrol, and who came with a delightful two-year-old daughter, Fiona. None of us left the act wealthy men and we all struggled to support our families. The combination of unscrupulous agents, managers and producers who often took advantage of our youth and naiveté assured that after 18 years in show business we three brothers had very little to show for it other than memories, a few scrapbooks, a pile of 45s, and two silver-tipped black dancing canes. I don't know where the other one went. I deeply regret missing out on a formal education, but it was an indisputable privilege to have been around for the era of Twice Nightly Variety. It was a time when performers had the opportunity to hone their act in front of an audience for 52 weeks a year, to polish jokes or songs or dance routines until they were as good as they could possibly get, where you had a chance to learn your profession, and to learn to be professional. It's a luxury that no longer exists.

According to Mike, I loved performing, had an incred-

THE KING BROTHERS

The King Brothers in 1968, attempting to look moody and cool (and failing).

ibly effervescent personality, an innocence, and was not remotely shy".

Perhaps this is true, I honestly don't know, but what I do know is that by the age of 30 my effervescence had lost quite a bit of its fizz. By then I knew what I wanted to do and it wasn't performing.

Let me tell you a little tale.

We once worked in Variety with a comedy dance act called The O'Keefe Brothers and Annette. Years later, after The King Brothers had gone their separate ways, Mike and I happened to be killing time together before a meeting at a London TV studio and were on our way down to the canteen for a cup of tea, when a pantomime cow passed us in the corridor.

"Hellooo, boys!" an Irish voice called out. We turned.

The cow took its head off and there stood Seamus O'Keefe, grinning broadly. "How're ye doin, lads?"

We greeted one another like old lost friends and tried to remember the various Hippodromes and Empires in which we'd worked together.

"How's – Annette?" Mike asked, tentatively, fearful she might have passed on by now.

"Here I am!" cried the rear end of the cow.

Annette went on to explain, through the spotted furry fabric, that since the death of Variety, their cow act had been their bread and butter. They both seemed pretty cheerful about it.

I knew then and there that whatever direction my life might take, we'd made the right decision in breaking up the act when we did, before The King Brothers ended their days in a third-rate touring production of *Peter Pan*, all three packed tightly into a crocodile suit.

Chapter 14

HORSES FOR COURSES

It's one thing to know what you want to do in life, but quite another to know how to go about it.

In the meantime, playing golf, might I just say, is an excellent way to procrastinate, something my first wife was always keen to point out as I'd head up to Finchley Golf Course for the fifth time that week. Of *course* I knew I should be doing other things, more lucrative things, more responsible things, especially as I now had a wife and child to support, but on I played, feeling guilty, but not quite guilty enough to stop, forever marvelling at how quickly the mind convinces itself that getting one's handicap down will somehow enable one to produce award-winning music for which people will fork over vast sums of money (and thereby get the new set of clubs I wanted). It was suggested, rather in the form that an ultimatum is suggested, that if I were truly serious about wanting to write film and television music for a living, then I should perhaps learn how to do it, and that the best place to do this might be at school. Thus, having not set foot inside a classroom since I was 15 (Christ Church Secondary School, Southport), it was more with trepidation than excitement that I enrolled at the Guildhall School of Music and Drama in London to study orchestration. I could only afford one term.

I suppose I had in mind a sort of crash course in scoring for orchestra. My tutor, an eminent classical composer named Professor Edmund Rubbra, thought otherwise. My first homework assignment (and, in fact, my last) was to get hold of a piano copy of Debussy's *La fille aux cheveux de lin*, take it home, and start scoring it for a full symphony orchestra. I'd never heard of the piece. Professor Rubbra had to repeat the name three times and play a snatch of it for me on the Bechstein before I finally said it sounded vaguely familiar, something which appeared to please him. On the way home, I bought a copy of the music, several sheets of score paper, two new HB pencils, a sharpener, a rubber, the latter of which proved to be particularly useful, and then with a certain amount of dread, because I'd never scored for anything other than piano, bass, guitar and drums, and once for a washboard, made a start.

I lived, ate, breathed (and erased) *La fille aux cheveux de lin*, solidly, for the whole week, at the end of which I had managed to complete only the first four bars. Somewhat embarrassed, I took my homework in to Professor Rubbra, who peered at it (this didn't take long) and asked why I had arranged the opening phrase for flute. I wasn't sure what he meant.

"Because I heard it that way," I said. Professor Rubbra smiled and shook his head.

"No, no, no, it has to be clarinet!"

"Oh," I said. "Why is that?"

138

"Because it always is," he explained.

"Oh," I said again. I still didn't know what he meant, but he was insistent and he was the professor, after all, while I was the former King Brother from Hornchurch who'd left school at 15 and had a few hit records – not to mention shared dressing rooms with, in no particular order, Jimi Hendrix, Alex the Juggling Nazi, and Marqueez and His Chattering Chimps – so when it came to having clarinets or not having clarinets, I accepted that Professor Rubbra had the definite edge on me. However, he never gave me a satisfactory explanation as to why it shouldn't be a flute and I think I was able to score two more bars of the piece over the next few weeks before we decided to drop the whole assignment.

I completed the term, just. Although I liked the Professor, we clearly didn't see eye-to-eye and probably never would, and I'm not sure what I got out of the course other than being able to put "Studied at The Guildhall School of Music, London" on my CV, which seems to impress people (you just don't mention the one term part).

About eight years earlier, while still performing as a King Brother, I wrote a song for the "B" side of one of our records called *Gotta Feeling*. It was the first song I'd ever written, both words and music (to this day my one and only success as a lyricist) and while it was nothing especially memorable, it went on to be recorded by Doris Day, which was enough to make me think I might have a future as a songwriter even though, deep down, writing for film and television was what I desperately wanted to do. By the time I'd enrolled at the Guildhall I'd already had a couple of television sitcom themes accepted, and this was encouraging, even though some-one else had orchestrated them, and I felt I could now legitimately call myself a composer.

Well, almost. To my way of thinking, a composer, as opposed to a songwriter, should first of all be someone who doesn't just pick out a melody on a keyboard or sing it into a tape recorder. Walter Scharf, Hollywood film composer, had to build the score for *Willy Wonka and the Chocolate Factory* based on rather primitive tape recordings created by songwriters Anthony Newley and Leslie Bricusse and he forever after referred to them, despite their accomplishments, as "The Hummers". A composer also ought to have the tools to know what to do with this melody once he's found it, and how to get the very best out of it. And, in order to do this, very simply, you need to know how to orchestrate, to be able to hear the sound of each instrument in your head and know how to commit that sound to paper or, these days, computer. The Guildhall patently wasn't the answer for me, so I knew I had somehow to figure it out for myself. Yet again, I was reminded that Finchley Golf Course was not really the answer, and that the first thing a budding television composer required, and I imagine this still holds true – was a job.

How you went about finding a job back then was you'd contact a television company and anyone you knew there, remind them you were a former King Brother ("Britain's Youngest Rhythm Aces!") and with that impressive pedigree in mind, ask them to please consider you for any future composing work. Your name went on a list (or in the bin) and you'd wait. If this was the BBC, occasionally a letter would arrive outlining details of a forthcoming show and inviting you to submit a theme tune. You would read the brief, make a cup of coffee, light a cigarette, sit down at the piano, fiddle around for an hour or two, say "Sod this for a game of darts!" and get up and go out and hit a few golf balls.

Thus inspired, you would return to the piano, knock out a couple of tunes, record them onto reel-to-reel tape and send it in along with a piano part on manuscript paper. Usually you'd never hear from them but if you were lucky, about three months later you'd get it all returned to you in the post with a note saying "Sorry, it was not what the producer was looking for." And, when the show would be transmitted, you'd look for the music credit, and there it would be, sure enough: "Music by Ronnie Hazlehurst", then Head of Music at BBC Television. You began to wonder if there was a connection. Be nice to think there wasn't, but the fact remained, you had a much better chance of success if you were dealing with ITV companies (and got better money).

One fine day, I learned from a music publisher friend of a new series about to go into production for London Weekend Television. It was about a horse.

Black Beauty, the 1877 novel by Anna Sewell, was being made into a children's adventure television series and the producers, Paul Knight and Sidney Cole, were in the market for a suitable theme tune. The brief was like any other brief that came my way – and a tune is a tune, you try your best whatever the project – but *The Adventures of Black Beauty*, as the series would be called, was already generating a lot of attention. The buzz was out that this one "would be big". Sixteen composers were being invited to submit.

"Strong outdoor theme à la *The Virginian*, but not cowboy or American and not less than 35 seconds" was all I had to go on, and with that brief brief in mind, I sat down at my piano, for once didn't get up, and an hour later had a melody I was happy with. I put it to one side

141

for 24 hours. When I went back to it, I was still happy with it and convinced it was what I wanted, so I tinkered a bit, made some adjustments, recorded it onto quarter-inch tape, and sent it off, along with a manuscript lead sheet, and waited – something that by then I was rather good at.

Within the week, Harry Rabinowitz, Head of Music at London Weekend Television, rang me.

"Denis? It's Harry. The producers have chosen eight out of the 16 submissions, and you're one of them!"

Four days later he rang again.

"Denis? It's Harry. The producers have chosen four out of the remaining eight, and you're one of them!"

A week later the phone rang again.

"Denis? It's Harry. Congratulations! They've chosen your theme!"

"That's fantastic, Harry!" I cried, looking around for someone to tell besides the dog.

"You do realise," Harry said, "that you'll be expected to compose and score all the incidental music as well? There are 52 episodes. That's an awful lot of music. You *are* capable of this. *Aren't you, Denis?*" he added, knowing full well how inexperienced I was but wanting me to succeed.

"Yes, of course, Harry!" I managed to say, lighting another Silk Cut to accompany the one I was already smoking. Of course I could do it! Why, what's 52 episodes of horse music for anyone who could master four bars of *La fille aux cheveux de lin*? Upwards and onwards! High Ho Silver!

The next shock was that the *Black Beauty* theme had to be recorded the following Saturday and I had five days to orchestrate it. It seems the studio and a 40-piece orchestra plus chorus had been booked for a Tommy Steele Special but Tommy had flu and London Weekend didn't want to waste the recording session. I cancelled a dinner party for my mother-in-law (not the greatest sacrifice), an evening at the theatre, with far deeper regret pulled out of a golf tournament at Moor Park, and opened a book called *Orchestration* by Walter Piston, which purported to be a sort of bible for serious composers, but I couldn't make head nor tail of it. It was about then that I started to panic.

I mentioned this to a friend of mine – actor, comedian, outstanding musician Dudley Moore, whom I ran into at the chemist's in Hampstead High Street, having nipped out for yet another packet of indigestion tablets, and an hour later there was a knock at my door. There was Dudley, having galloped over to the rescue with a gift for me, a book called *Sounds and Scores* by Henry Mancini. It saved me.

If ever you want to know about orchestration, anything at all, how to do it, what it's all about, what's the range of an oboe or a French horn, what are the two longest glisses you can get from a trombone, any normal everyday questions, you should consider investing in this book. It has proved indispensable to me and even after 40 years (I've had it rebound, twice) I still occasionally refer to it. Mancini makes his guide accessible to the novice, easy to understand, and removes a lot of the mystery. Most important, he shows you how to have confidence. As did Dudley, who was always happy to pop round to advise a fledgling orchestrator.

Thus armed with Henry M, my pencils, and trusty rubber, I got my head down and scored the full theme for *The Adventures of Black Beauty* which London Weekend Television would later re-title *Galloping Home*. I also scored what are known as the "opening and closing titles" and the "in and out of commercials", all for a 40-piece orchestra and chorus, and all was recorded at Wembley Studios in May of 1972 with Harry Rabinowitz conducting the "London String Chorale" (a made-up name for the record release) and me watching anxiously from the control room with the producers Paul and Sid. It would be another couple of years before I would be confident enough to buy a baton and wave my arms about in front of people who, frankly, can spot a phony a mile off.

The recording went well. Harry Rabinowitz congratulated me, so did many of the musicians. Paul Knight was positively euphoric. More importantly, the orchestration seemed to work. Miraculously, I hadn't screwed up! I hadn't given the second violins an F Sharp instead of an F, everyone loved the French horns going BRUUUP! BRUUUP! It all worked. I'd actually done it! Amazing.

I decided I'd never let the Mancini book out of my sight, and invited Dudley and his wife for Christmas.

Composing the incidental or background music for *The Adventures of Black Beauty* proved something of an adventure itself – it was a considerably more complicated operation than scoring the theme. I had never experienced synchronising music to film, never seen anyone do it, and didn't know how on earth it was done.

It was done, at least it was in 1972, I soon discovered, with something called a Moviola, a free-standing machine about the size of a large tumble dryer but looking more like a Heath Robinson combination film projector, cash register and slot machine. The one I first encountered resided in the cutting room at London Weekend Television, and therein lay the bulk of the problem.

Posing with a borrowed Moviola machine, trying to score the background music for The Adventures of Black Beauty, *1973. The hair and sideboards are my own.*

In a half-hour episode, there would typically be an average of 15 minutes of background music, all of which had to be specially written for each individual episode and tailored to the action on screen. As a general rule, you'd be required to write lyrical music for a pastoral scene, jolly music for a happy one, dramatic for moments of high drama and so on – and all connected in this case by what seemed hours and hours of endless, incessant, galloping hooves. Which music went where was discussed and decided by the director, the film editor, and me, and this discussion took place in the cutting room in front of the Moviola, on which footage of the episode could be seen on a tiny viewing screen. Imagine three heads crammed together all trying to peer at one iPhone and you'll get the picture.

The director of the first episode was Charles Crichton, famous for Ealing comedies and later *A Fish Called Wanda*, and also famous for smoking his pipe throughout the editing sessions, thus creating an atmosphere akin to London smog in the enclosed quarters of the cutting room. We'd watch the entire episode (or what we could see of it) then watch it again, but this time stopping and starting while the editor and I took notes and critical timings with our stopwatches. When we were all agreed as to what kind of music was required where, I would go home, but not, unfortunately, with the magnificent Moviola machine. I would have just a sheet of paper covered with my hastily scribbled notes and timings to refer to, the idea being that I would be able to decipher the whole thing, once on my own, and that I'd also remember every single frame of a film I had seen twice, at most, from a remote angle, and be able to compose appropriate music to fit. From the outset, I spotted the odd gaping hole in this spectacular theory.

First of all, within a three-minute film sequence there might be five or six or more dramatic points that needed musical underlining – a door opens and the villain appears, Vicky leaps onto Beauty, villain brandishes a stick, Beauty rears up, Vicky falls off Beauty and so on. And, of course, it was vital that the underscore be synchronised to these moments to within a fraction of a second. This is something that nowadays is comparatively easy to accomplish with video, DVDs, computers and click tracks at one's disposal but not so easy then, with only a stopwatch and a wind-up metronome.

Secondly, to expect outstanding results from a memory that has been severely tested a number of times, not always successfully, by the complexities of travel directions, shopping lists, or the arrival of a new colour scheme in the

The cover of the sheet music of my theme for the television series The Adventures of Black Beauty, *which opened doors in 1972.*

hallway is, well, optimistic to say the least. With my metronome ticking back and forth, I sat at my piano counting bars, counting seconds, trying to make sense of my notes, desperately trying to remember what the hell I'd seen earlier – was this her getting on the horse or off the horse?

Or the horse rearing up? Or had it already done that? Or Christ! Maybe the horse had already bolted! The whole process was torture and, I can say this now, I don't much care for horses anyway and was certainly sick of them by the end of 52 episodes.

Half an hour before the first recording session at Olympic Studios for the incidental music for Episode One, Harry Rabinowitz, who would be conducting the orchestra, met me in the hallway outside the control room to have a quick look at my scores, which I handed over rather reluctantly, then awaited with the same sense of doom I'd experienced outside Father Andrew's study at St. Bonaventure's Grammar School, Forest Gate.

"Cue One and Cue Seven," Harry said. "The stable-hands' fistfight and the horses over the hedgerows. There's not enough music (how could he know so quickly!) but don't worry!" Harry gave me a friendly pat and headed for the studio. "I'll make it work."

And he did. The session started, the film clip for the first cue came up on the big screen, the musicians started playing my music, and Harry, by conducting it slower here and faster there, made it all fit perfectly and sound magnificent to boot. And I was getting all the credit! How marvellous! I liked this composing lark, composing was fun!

Harry Rabinowitz's kindness and, I have to say, genius, carried on throughout the recording of the entire series. There is nothing better than practical experience and being thrown in at the deep end is often the best thing that can happen. But his kindness didn't stop in the studios, after every morning session we'd retire to his office at London Weekend TV where he'd take me through the scores, bar by bar, while listening to the audio tape of what we'd just recorded, and he'd show me how to improve things. For instance, I had at one point used a solo flute (the very one that Professor Rubbra wouldn't let me use) under Vicky's dialogue. Harry pointed out that as the flute was in the same register as Vicky's voice, I would be better off using an instrument with a lower pitch, one that would complement it, such as a cello. Brilliant, I thought! I learned more from Harry Rabinowitz in the average afternoon than if I'd stayed at the Guildhall for the rest of my life.

To date, *The Adventures of Black Beauty* has earned me more in royalties than anything I've ever written. It continues to be transmitted all over the world, the theme has been used for commercials, ring tones, the news, practically any time there's horseracing on television and, my personal favourite, it featured in an episode of the sitcom *I'm Alan Partridge* as "music to party by" in a motel room. The music won an Ivor Novello Award for Best TV Theme and in a national newspaper poll was voted the second most memorable TV theme of all time, just being pipped at the post by my mother's all-time favourite, *Hawaii Five-O*. Book 'em, Beauty. Murder one, three counts.

Chapter 15

TWO'S COMPANY

One October morning, I got a phone call from my music publisher, David Platz, asking if I'd be interested in working with the legendary American lyricist Sammy Cahn. This is like asking my brother Tony if he'd fancy a round with Tiger Woods. *All The Way, Come Fly With Me, Call Me Irresponsible, High Hopes, Three Coins In The Fountain*, the list of Sammy's hits goes on and on. Four Oscars and 23 nominations, Golden Globes, Emmys, Grammys... Cahn was the master.

"David?" I said, "not only would I clear my appointment calendar to meet – let alone work – with Sammy Cahn, I think I'd be willing to marry him."

London Weekend Television was producing a new comedy series called *Two's Company* starring Elaine Stritch and Donald Sinden and wanted an original song for the opening and closing credits. David Platz, also LWT's music publisher, told me that they'd need the song recorded within the next two weeks and that Sammy

Cahn had only a brief window in which we could meet and work. En route from Paris to New York, he'd be staying overnight at Claridge's on the Friday and available the following morning.

Excited, and without even a glance towards my golf clubs, I started my homework, read the script, liked it, and although this second I could sing for you pretty much every song Sammy Cahn has ever written, backwards, forwards and probably inside out – over the next two days, for inspiration, I listened non-stop to Sinatra albums. I knew the kind of tune I wanted to write, I knew the tempo, the style and the structure, and sat down at the piano.

The process of creating a melody is a mysterious thing. Sometimes it just happens, sometimes it doesn't, and sometimes you're sorry you ever said yes to the project in the first place, but in this case it came to me right away, in fact twice. In an hour and a half I'd written two tunes and liked them both, but would Sammy?

By the time I drove up to Claridge's at 11 o'clock on the Saturday morning, 15 minutes early, Sammy was already pacing the lobby. I recognised him instantly, having seen his one-man show the previous year. Short, bald, glasses, moustache, and never still – always darting here and there like a wind-up toy on wheels. Sammy carried a newspaper, had a Burberry mac slung over his arm and wore tan trousers, a blue shirt, and a grey cardigan. I'm now sorry I've just written that because my second wife (in fact, my first one did, too) says I never notice wardrobe detail (all the more reason to have married Sammy Cahn instead).

In any event, I paused, successfully resisting the urge to throw myself at his tan-tasselled-loafer-clad feet and tell him how much I loved his lyric for *The Second*

Time Around, then introduced myself.

"Hey, how are ya?" he said, already heading towards the revolving door. "Where we goin'?"

I hurried to catch up and off we drove in my brown two-door Lancia (with the hideous, bilious green upholstery, my wife has just added) to Essex Studios in central London. On the way, making conversation, I asked if he'd had time to read the script.

"Nah, I know what they want," he said with a wave of his hand. "No problem."

At the studio, a piano, two chairs, a yellow legal pad and two sharpened pencils awaited us. Except for the sound engineer, we were the only ones there. Sammy made a beeline for the pad and one of the pencils.

"So whatcha got for me?"

"Oh... right," I said, thinking what, no coffee first? No general badinage about the intricacies of song writing? How to achieve the perfect rhyme? The juxtaposition of lyrical imagery with musical cadence? More important, what's Sinatra really like to work with?

I moved to the piano, sat down, and launched into Tune Number One. After a few bars he stopped me.

"Hey I like that. Play that bit again." Sammy started scribbling. (He likes it! He likes it!)

"Play samore," he said, so I did, and by the time I'd got to the end of the tune he was finishing the last words of his lyric. He ripped off the sheet of paper and handed it to me.

"Can ya sing it?"

I played and sang *Two's Company*. Sammy Cahn's words were spot-on perfect. Witty, beautifully rhymed, the lyric fitted the Elaine Stritch and Donald Sinden characters to a tee – she a brassy American writer living in London, and he her snooty English butler. The whole operation took approximately 10 minutes, after which Sammy said: "Ya got anything else?", so I played him Tune Number Two and the process repeated itself, this time resulting in a lyric with a completely different approach but equally perfect. I had him back at Claridge's within 45 minutes. We said goodbye, he went off to the airport, and I drove home to Hampstead, dazed and euphoric, feeling extremely pleased with myself until my then wife asked: "Where's the dog?" (the answer being "still at the vet's", I'd forgotten to collect him), and also if I'd remembered to pick up the flowers she'd ordered for my mother's birthday (the answer being "no").

At London Weekend Television the following Tuesday, I sang and played both Cahn/King songs for Michael Grade, then Head of Light Entertainment, Humphrey Barclay the producer, the director Stuart Allen, and Elaine Stritch, who clearly had the final say. She said she was happy with either song and asked which one I preferred. I chose Tune Number One, everyone seemed pleased, Elaine said how much she was looking forward to recording it in a week's time, and we all went on our merry way.

And so, over the next few days, I wrote the arrangement, booked the studio, booked the orchestra, and took the score to my copyist John Evans. He returned it on the day of the session and I drove up to CTS Studios in Wembley in time for the 7pm start. I rehearsed the orchestra, then recorded the backing track – the music track Elaine and Donald would sing to later – so that everything was ready for the two stars' scheduled arrival at 8pm at which point we could release the band (send them home), which we duly did. I had just enough time, by my reckoning, for a quick cup of tea and a biscuit, both of which I enjoyed thoroughly, blissfully unaware that an evening recording session was perhaps not the best idea if Miss Stritch were involved.

Donald Sinden arrived at the appointed hour. Charming, but unbearably nervous, he professed to not having a musical bone in his body. I assured him that this wasn't a problem, that he wouldn't have to sing, as such, he could just "speak it", the important thing was that he had to come in on the right beat – a skill that would prove to be an even greater hurdle than his inability to pitch the note. However, our main concern for the time being was the fact that there was no sign of Elaine. We all began to get a tad twitchy, especially the director, as the clock ticked on. Just after 9pm, the control room door banged open.

Elaine Stritch stood there – just about – swaying, swigging from a bottle in a brown paper bag and hanging onto her husband, who, in turn, was hanging onto her, both of them clearly plastered.

Nobody moved. I'm trying to remember if I even breathed.

Elaine then bravely let go of her husband. She stumbled, staggered, grabbed onto the control desk, pulled herself up, looked round the room, spotted the director Stuart Allen and snarled: "Whash *he* doing here?" – and before he or any of us could explain, she pointed her finger at him and said: "Why doanchew fuckoff!"

There was an uncomfortable pause.

Stuart mumbled something like "I say, Miss Stritch, please!", at which point she repeated her instruction, which he then followed, red with embarrassment and or rage. I could see Donald Sinden through the glass, in the studio, frantically practising his words in order to come in on the right beat, or indeed any beat. The engineer and I exchanged an uneasy glance. The prospect of successfully recording a duet with a sozzled star who could barely speak let alone sing, and Donald, who clearly couldn't count, seemed highly unlikely.

"Well!" I said, with a huge, if unconvincing, smile. "Are we all ready to give it a go? What do you think?"

Elaine turned and tried hard to focus on me.

"Yeahwhynot," she said, eventually, and allowed me to guide her gracefully into the studio where Donald waited, sweating, in front of the microphone. I helped Elaine precariously onto a stool and handed her the sheet of lyrics. She mumbled "Thanksh". For reasons unknown, she appeared to have taken a sort of shine to me. At least I was not ordered to, er, take my leave, and I took that as a good sign.

I managed to place a pair of headphones on her and keep them there, no small feat, as her head kept lolling to one side. Donald was already wearing his (they allow the performers to hear the music track which they, in theory, sing along to). Perhaps he was distracted by the sheer terror of having to count and sing at the same time or perhaps, like a true English gent, he was simply behaving as if there were nothing amiss, but he didn't appear to notice his co-star sliding gently off the stool next to him.

After helping Elaine back up – and exchanging a few more cheerful glances through the glass with the sound engineer – I donned my own headphones and took my place directly in front of the two stars, ready to conduct, cue, and catch, as necessary. The red light went on. The music track started.

And then, a metamorphosis occurred. Elaine's head shot up. Her whole body straightened, her eyes suddenly sparkled, she opened her mouth and, at exactly the right moment, without me even cueing her, she sang Sammy Cahn's lyric, note perfect, in character, with flair and humour and everything else one could have hoped for, and, had it not been for Donald's inability to locate the beat, we would have had the recording in the can after that first take. Elaine was that good. And she was that good on the five subsequent takes, but between each one, she would slump back down on the stool and become incoherent again. I've never seen anything like it.

Two's Company ran for four series from 1975 to 1979. A year later Sammy Cahn and I wrote another song together for another Elaine Stritch sitcom, *Nobody's Perfect*. The lyric was never used in the end, but we continued to correspond. The last time I saw Sammy was in New York in 1980 at his apartment on East 68th Street.

"Come in, come in, hello my chum from England!" Sammy ushered me in. "Hey, you want some *tea?*" he asked before closing the front door and beetling out of sight around the corner, presumably in the direction of tea. I followed. The place was almost bare. What was left of the furniture was covered in sheets, paintings were stacked against the wall, with things in plastic packaging piled everywhere.

"Ehhh, I'm goin' through a divorce," Sammy said, dismissing the state of the place. "Hey! Hey! Wanna hear what I wrote for Sinatra? He's singin' it at the White House!"

I pursued him down a corridor and into a room where I found Sammy already seated at a piano. There was a rickety-looking wooden folding chair in the corner and I perched on it as Sammy, bursting with enthusiasm, launched into a parody of *All The Way* that he'd written for Sinatra to sing at Ronald Reagan's Inaugural Gala in

157

Washington DC. It was witty and clever, as expected, and I smiled appreciatively throughout. Mostly, though, I enjoyed watching *Sammy* appreciate his own cleverness and wit.

"Did ya like that line? Isn't that a good line? Frank's gonna love it!"

After we'd discussed at length the excellence of the parody and I was just about ready for that promised cup of tea, to enjoy my wooden folding chair more thoroughly, Sammy looked at his watch and leapt up.

"Geez! You gotta get outta here, Frank's due here in five minutes to rehearse!" Sammy shooed me towards the door.

"Frank?" I said, making a grab for my coat as I was propelled past a bubble-wrapped sofa. *The* Frank? Frank the Man?

"You can't be here when Frank's here! He doesn't like strangers."

Strangers! Hardly. "Excuse me, Mr. Sinatra. Don't you remember me from the Festival Hall in '62? You said 'Hi kid!' to me as you left the stage?"

I couldn't just sit quietly on the folding chair and watch rehearsal? Frank would like that, or hide in the closet and listen, maybe pop out to surprise him at the end?

Alas, I was hustled into the lift, sans tea and sans catching sight of Ol' Blue Eyes, but Sammy and I kept in touch for many years. We were always on the lookout for a stage project to do together but the right one never came up. His typed letters were warm, chatty and complimentary, and he amused himself by, every time the letter combination "C O N" appeared, replacing it with "Cahn", C A H N, capital C, as in "a large Cahn-tingent" or "in our last Cahn-versation".

"One of these days," he wrote, in the last letter I had from him before he died, "we may find ourselves back downstairs at Essex writing our little hearts out in that recording studio! On that happy thought and with 'high hopes' for all your endeavours on your Cahn-tinent, I am your good chum, Sammy."

Chapter 16

"FIN SWING – KING!"

Goran the Swedish record producer came into my life after my theme for a TV series called *We'll Meet Again* about American pilots in Britain during World War II went "gold" in Sweden. No need for fireworks here, it only means it sold 50,000 copies, but it's fun to have a gold record on your wall (you just hang it up high so no one can read the Sweden and the 50,000 part). The Swedish for "We'll Meet Again" is "Vi Mots Igen" and represents the full extent of my Scandinavian vocabulary except for a phrase taught to me by my wife Astrid – one which I have found essential over my years of visiting the Land of the Midnight Sun – and that is "Nei takk, jeg liker ikke sild!" which means "No, thank you, I don't like herring!"

Goran's command of English was far better than my Swedish but he took his time with it, speaking at the rate of approximately eight words per minute (Astrid timed him once). The phone would ring.

"Hello?" you'd say, then wait. Pick up a book. Trim your cuticles. Make a cup of coffee. The big hope was that Goran didn't ring while we were out so I'd have to ring him back at my expense.

"Oh!" he'd say, eventually, and sounding surprised that you answered at your own number. Then, about a year later: "Hello!" And then, finally, as if there could be even the slightest doubt as to whom this accent belonged: "Diss iss Sveden calling!"

Besides producing the gold record, which Astrid figured we'd be melting any day in order to cover our phone bill, Goran had devised a money-making scheme (for him, not us, as it turned out) whereby I would create a series of albums for the Swedish market featuring Big Band Glenn Miller-type dance music, to consist mostly of old standards but also some original material, songs and instrumentals, all to be arranged and conducted by me, recorded in London, and performed by the 'Denis King Orchestra' and sung by the 'Denis King Singers', none of whom actually existed, except me, obviously. Astrid said she thought this sounded like a hitch until I explained that all I had to do was get on the phone and book a great line-up of session musicians and singers, as I would, say, for a commercial or TV recording, and I could call them what I wanted.

Goran insisted that two or three tracks of old Swedish favourites be included on each album, such as *Räkna de lyckliga stunderna blott* and (you'll remember this one) *Den killen ar crazy*, all of which drove me crazy with their tunelessness – not to mention their spellings. Goran also wanted old-fashioned posed album covers à la "Hey We're the DK Big Band Don't We Look Spiffy", which required group shots in various photographer's studios with the band in black tie sitting behind cardboard music stands with big silver DKs on them, smiling and holding their instruments. The session singers, myself included, also had to be decked out as if for an American high-school prom, grouped happy and finger-snapping in the foreground.

"You'd buy ten of these without hearing a note," Astrid said, rolling her eyes. But when the first album came out, called *Dance In The Old-Fashioned Way*, Sweden, for reasons passing all understanding, became gripped by DENIS KING! mania. Of course, we're

One of my big-band albums for the Swedish market, this one translated as Sweet Souvenirs. *I appear here with Nick Curtis, Norma Winstone, Tracy Miller, and the boys in the band. The year was 1990 but the producer wanted a 1940s feel. If you think this cover is corny, you should see the other ones.*

talking here about a low-key Scandinavian sort of mania, not quite on a par with, say, an ELVIS! mania, but just take it that a fair number of Swedes were going around muttering "Ja, diss moosic iss vehry nice" with zero inflection and only if asked.

"FIN SWING – KING!" says one headline above what I'm assuming is a glowing newspaper review, one of many, as Goran immediately started on about me coming to Sweden myself to do publicity for the album and to "perform in the awtenum". It took us three weeks to figure out he meant October and not some nightclub in Stockholm, and awtenum had indeed turned into vinter-um by the time Astrid and I were loading four days' worth of interview outfits into the car and heading to Heathrow.

Sweden in October, I can report, is dark and cold and full of snow. I have in front of me a photo taken for a local magazine of a happy, smiling Denis King and his "sambo", a curious Swedish term for a living-together-but-not-married partner. We are posing in a snow-covered downtown square, Astrid looking tall and regal in a fur coat and high-heeled boots and me next to her looking small and slightly less regal and, I've just this minute noticed, standing on tiptoe.

For two days I did what seemed like dawn-to-dusk interviews (although dusk at that time of the year seems to take up most of the day) and non-stop record signings, unable to believe the crowds lined up at a department store were for me and not for some new food processor demonstration. While Astrid darted off here and there to purchase items she assured me we couldn't live without such as three dozen glögg cups, an assortment of wooden trays with heart cut-outs and armful after armful of red candles, I scribbled "Best Wishes to Sven-Petter!"

and so on, as a queue of excited (but very in control) Swedes snaked out into the street.

The following year, 1984, Goran decided he wanted to bring over not just me but the whole of my Big Band, so in mid-December, Astrid and I, by now married and no longer sambo material, found ourselves on an 8am flight to Malmo aboard a specially-chartered 40-seater turbo-prop 748 flying machine, with three singers, 17 musicians and their instruments and we'd no sooner taken off than the Denis King Orchestra was heavily into Duty Free. Astrid and I sat up front like school prefects on a field trip, indulging our brood, and making up answers to their various questions about things we knew nothing about, such as filming TV shows in Malmo and what time we'd be landing. Four seats next to us had had to be removed so that Lennie Bush's double bass (which he wouldn't let out of his sight) could have a seatbelt, but he then discovered it was in the non-smoking section so we kept having to bass sit, promising to guard it with our lives, as if the flight attendants were going to steal it, while Lennie, practically a 12-carton-a-day man, went aft to smoke a few packs.

The turbo-prop flew at roughly the same speed as the passing seagulls and about two feet above the water, but the absolutely sensational news was that Malmo – as the pilot reported over the PA system, but which no one could hear due to rowdy musician noise, so Astrid stuck her head into the cockpit and said "WHAT?" – was fogged in, so we circled. Eventually, some of the band noticed this and lurched forward to ask what was happening.

Fog, apparently a good excuse for drinks all round, had also descended over Copenhagen, but not as badly. Nonetheless, they were threatening to close the airport unless we got there fast, so in we flapped, landing three hours late in the wrong country, leaving large numbers of people at Swedish TV in Malmo gleefully filling in their overtime claims, and with 17 musicians getting progressively more legless.

So there we were, parked on the runway in wonderful, wonderful Copenhagen, with everyone, including the pilot, wondering what to do, and the band arguing loudly as to what would go better with pickled herring, Dubonnet or lager, when suddenly: message from Malmo! And it's grab your coat, don't forget your hat, leave your worries on the doorstep and we're hustled across the Tarmac and into the terminal where Astrid and I steered the boys clear of the bar in the transit lounge and raced everyone plus the double bass onto a chartered Danish coach which then screeched across town to catch a waiting ferry boat named *Hamlet*.

The band discovered yet more beer on the boat, then it was full speed onto a Swedish coach which, according to a note I had been handed by someone in a uniform on *Hamlet*, was to "Rendezvous at customs barrier with Mrs. Anderson in blow Volvo", which Astrid helpfully translated as "blue Volvo". In no time at all we were rolling up at Malmo TV in time for the dinner break, which made about our 10th meal so far, since everyone had been feeding us to make up for fog.

The band was, dare I say, not necessarily in the best shape for rehearsals, a number of them needing help just to make it up the two steps to the cardboard bandstands, most of which immediately toppled over, due to musicians grabbing onto them for support. This, I thought to myself, is the band Sweden's been holding its breath for.

"Der television people are wehry worried about der taping tomorrow," Goran said, in case we'd missed this.

We were then all bussed into town to a hotel, which was wehry nice but, disappointingly for the band, had no bar, and so those who were still able to stand peeled off into the darkness, only to be further disappointed to find

Imagine a world in which my music is more popular than Lennon's, Michael Jackson's, or Sinatra's – and you have Sweden in 1983.

the only place open was a branch of McDonalds. Astrid and I, meanwhile, being Den Mothers, quietly shared a 7-UP from a machine in the one-sofa-one-chair lobby before the excitement finally became too much and we trundled off to our eiderdowns.

The next morning at breakfast we were unspeakably bright-eyed and Astrid tried to see how many musicians she could nauseate by eating herring at their table.

The idea of this TV show was that DK and his jaunty band are entertaining everyone at a Swedish night club, what Sweden perhaps thinks the Rainbow Room in Rockefeller Center looks like. The set featured a vaguely art deco New York skyline with, according to Astrid who knows about these things, "heavy use of Mylar", a shiny reflective material, and there seemed to be a lot of camera-panning through potted palms and bar glasses and close-ups of me singing at the piano with, again according to Astrid, busy keeping tabs on All Things Visual – an out-of-focus scotch bottle next to my head. Professional ballroom dancers had been hired to play the part of ordinary night-clubbers whooping it up on a Saturday night and these 10 or so couples, dripping with marabou and sequins, dipped, lunged, quick-stepped and fast-head-turned through shots in characteristic Swedish let-your-hair-down style, not smiling once. A Bafta Award surely beckoned.

The host was a well-known Swedish personality named Smoke-Rings Anderson. Rotund, dour, with a gravelly voice, he looked not unlike a bearded, Swedish version of Charles Laughton, only less attractive, and he injected razor-sharp Swedish humour into the scripted song intros.

"Denis, hello! Could you please tell us the name of the first song you are going to do for us tonight?"

"Of course. *PLEASED TO MEET YOU.*"

"Well, I am pleased to meet you too, Denis, but what is the name of the song?"

"*PLEASED TO MEET YOU.*"

"As I joost said, I am pleased to meet you too, *but tell me the name of the song!*"

"The name of the song *is PLEASED TO MEET YOU.*" (You big Swedish meatball.)

"Ohh… a yoke! I see! Ho ho ho!"

(BOTH LAUGH UNCONTROLLABLY. CUT TO CAMERA LURKING NEAR ICE BUCKET)

There was a Swedish man with earphones who kept walking around saying: "Vi go again!" He was quite possibly the director, but was never formally introduced and certainly never gave me or the singers any direction, so we had to wing it until Astrid stepped in on the sly, in case Earphones and Smoke-Rings didn't care for Fin Swing King's wife horning in, because she could see on the monitor that Tracy and Norma had palm frond shadows across their faces making them seem to be growing beards, and that I'd been looking like a Hobbit next to Nick, who was six foot one, especially as Nick was standing on the platform and I wasn't.

Now here's an odd thing. It would seem that musicians who've been drunk as a skunk the night before, can still play okay the next day.

Well, mostly.

Everything musically about the television recording went tickcty-boo until we got to the trombone solo in the middle section of *A Nightingale Sang In Berkeley Square*, at which point it became evident that the trombonist, normally a fine player, was having considerable difficulty not only finding the right notes but also which end of the slide to use.

After seven or eight takes with increasingly disastrous results, and with Goran anxiously checking his watch, no doubt worrying about yet more overtime and propellers starting to whir over at Malmo Airport – Earphones approached with Goran in tow to have a quiet word with me at the piano. It was suggested that we go ahead and do a take with whatever noise my trombonist was able to muster, and his solo would be redubbed later by a Swedish player. I said fine. We raced through the rest of the prog-ramme, packed up our gear, scooped up the trombonist and hurried off to the airport.

Malmo was clear of fog, hurrah, the band made the inevitable beeline for more Duty Free plus some presents for the wife and kids and then it was back on board The Little Airplane That Could (we hoped). Soon everyone was having *the* best time, no one in his seat (except us school monitors), some wearing orange life vests as shorts, Roy Willox wearing a red clown nose and playing "yakkity" (silly) sax up and down the aisle, and one of the trumpet players commandeering the PA system to do his Douglas Bader impersonation and perform several "This is your captain speaking" routines. The two flight attendants shut themselves in the toilet.

When *Smoke-Ring's Rainbow Room*, as it was called, was finally dubbed and edited, Goran sent us a video of the Denis King Big Band's Swedish television debut. Absolutely stunning, as expected, a veritable collector's item, the highlight for me being saxophonist Ray Swinfield's widening stare during the trombone solo on *A Nightingale Sang In Berkeley Square*. The disastrous solo had indeed been redubbed by a Swedish player, as promised, and sounded fine, but if you watch closely as the solo starts, you can clearly see Ray, seated directly below, adopting the pained expression of a man who has just been subjected to an appalling bout of flatulence.

Tragically, on the night *Smoke-Ring's Rainbow Room* was due to go out on Swedish national TV, Olof Palme, the Swedish Prime Minister, was assassinated, perhaps being mistaken for an English trombone player, and the transmission was postponed indefinitely. I imagine my copy of it would be worth a great deal should it ever turn up on *The Antiques Road Show* but I refuse to part with it.

After five albums, Goran and Sweden, amazingly, had had enough of the Denis King Big Band, and Goran stopped calling. We rather miss him. Every so often the phone rings, you say "Hello?", there's a pause, and for one marvellous moment you think Goran has found you again despite changing your number three times, but it turns out to be either someone from "Haitch Ess Bee Cee" bank or a British Gas call centre in Mumbai.

Chapter 17

THERE IS NOTHING LIKE A LAWSUIT

During the 10-year period leading up to 1986, I'd written well over 100 jingles for radio and television advertising – some won awards, some were instantly forgettable, and one got me into a lot of trouble, in fact virtually put an end to what had been a lucrative career as a jingles writer. The tale revolves around a London advertising agency called The Pearson Partnership, a company whose offices, I hear, burned to the ground a few years back. That was a distressing piece of news, mainly because I'd wanted to be the one to light the match.

I was commissioned by the aforementioned ad agency to write a parody of *There Is Nothing Like A Dame*, Rodgers and Hammerstein's well-known song from the musical *South Pacific*. It was for a big new television advertising campaign they were about to launch for National Express Coaches UK. A bus company.

Prior to contacting me, the Pearson Partnership had approached Chappell Music Publishers, who represent

Rodgers and Hammerstein's work in the UK, to ask permission to use the original song. Chappell refused, and I got the call. By then I had built up a bit of a reputation in the advertising business for parodying well-known works. I knew what you could get away with and what you couldn't, how "close" you could get, and at what point you'd get into trouble. To the uninitiated, this means being able to write a new melody in the style of the original melody but without infringing copyright.

I accepted the commission, as normal.

The campaign was to be called *You've Just Got To Meet Elaine*, Elaine being a cheery National Express Rapide Coach stewardess who smiles and hands out pillows to passengers during which a men's chorus whistles and sings lustily.

The "copy", or lyrics, had already been written by someone at The Pearson Partnership, someone who clearly should not have considered leaving his position as tea boy, but you take what you're given, and this is what I was given. [At the risk of making Oscar Hammerstein spin in his grave, sing these lyrics to the tune of *There Is Nothing Like A Dame*, beginning with the verse.]

WE'VE GOT COFFEE, WE'VE GOT TEA,
WE'VE GOT TOILETS IF NEED BE,
WE'VE GOT FILMS ON VIDEO
SO THERE'S LOTS FOR YOU TO SEE
WE'VE GOT SEATS SO YOU CAN LAY BACK
JUST LIKE THEY DO IN PLANES
AND BEST OF ALL, RAPIDE'S GOT ELAINE!
YOU'VE JUST GOT TO MEET ELAINE
SHE'S A REAL SWELL GIRL
YOU WOULD HAVE TO BE INSANE
TO CHOOSE ANYONE BUT RAPIDE'S ELAINE!

I can certainly understand Chappell's reluctance in allowing The Pearson Partnership anywhere near Rodgers and Hammerstein's celebrated work, but the last thing a composer's job in the world of advertising entails is criticism of the "copy" (at least to the copywriter's face). The commission was, in truth, rather a tricky one from my point of view. While creating a parody on words is comparatively easy to do, it's not so easy to make a recognisable parody of a melody within the space of a few seconds of TV time and, in this case, because The Pearson Partnership was insisting on a sung male chorus, with whistling, this would bring it even closer to the original.

My first effort was rejected out of hand by the creative team on the grounds that it wasn't "close enough" to *There Is Nothing Like A Dame*. I reminded them how very careful we had to be here. They said they knew that, but asked me to have another go, which I did, which was again rejected on the same grounds. I said we were stepping into a minefield if we got any closer. The Pearson Partnership assured me everything was fine, I should lose no sleep, they had a distinguished music copyright lawyer on board, a QC who would examine my composition and put his official stamp of approval on it before it was broadcast.

I rewrote *You've Just Got To Meet Elaine* for the third time, but felt uneasy about it.

Version Three of *Elaine* came dangerously close, in my opinion, to *There Is Nothing Like A Dame*. Note for note my melody was nothing like Richard Rodgers', but what with a big orchestra, a male chorus, and whistling, the end result would leave not a semblance of a doubt in the listener's mind as to what was the inspiration. Which in a way is what you want, and it's certainly what The Pearson Partnership wanted, and indeed were delighted with, but I knew that Chappell Music, especially having been approached initially, would be on the alert. Which indeed they turned out to be. The distinguished music copyright Queens Counsel gave his full approval to Version Three and we recorded it, I swear, on April Fool's Day, 1986. Once the completed track had been delivered, I was asked by The Pearson Partnership to sign a Letter of Indemnity, which I willingly did, stating that *You've Just Got To Meet Elaine* was an original work of mine. Letters of indemnity are common practice in the field of musical composition; you don't usually get the job unless you're prepared to sign one. I honestly thought nothing of it.

The Pearson Partnership shot their film to my track and a jolly commercial of singing and whistling men on a National Express Rapide coach being handed pillows and shown where the toilets were by a beaming, smartly-uniformed Elaine debuted on Channel 4 on the 5th of May, Bank Holiday Monday, at 8.45 in the evening.

At 10.10pm my phone rang. "Denis? We have problems."

It was somebody from The Pearson Partnership whose name I don't remember and don't care.

"Just had a call from Chappell's. They want us to take the commercial off the air. They consider it a complete infringement of copyright!" His tone indicated that somehow this was my fault.

"So what am I supposed to do about it?"

"We'll discuss it in the morning. They're threatening an injunction. We're going to have a meeting!" He hung up, ensuring me a blissful night's sleep.

At the meeting, to which I was not invited, The Pearson Partnership, acting upon the advice of the distinguished music copyright QC who said my music for the commercial was by no means an infringement of copyright, it was merely "an affectionate parody", made the decision to keep *You've Just Got To Meet Elaine* on the air and ignore Chappell's threat of injunction. Another 76 broadcasts went out. Chappell Music, now joined by the Rodgers and Hammerstein Estate, with the backing of the Performing Rights Society, decided to sue The Pearson Partnership and National Express for infringement of copyright. A court date was set for the 13th of June. The knowledge that I was going to be called as a principal defence witness in the High Court initiated a move on my part from Ovaltine to Valium. Harder still was coming to terms with the fact that Rodgers and Hammerstein, who had always been my heroes, were suddenly the enemy. I was only marginally reassured by the fact that in a survey the QC had arranged the previous week at a shopping mall in Birmingham whereby out of 137 shoppers invited into a room to hear the jingle, only four said it reminded them of *There Is Nothing Like A Dame*. Other answers ranged from "The Beatles" (which was nice) to "Rachmaninov" (which was even nicer) to someone who just put down "Smith".

It was explained to me, by the distinguished music copyright QC, that along with providing a detailed affidavit analysing melody, harmonic and rhythm accompaniment in general, my evidence would involve a live performance in court on a keyboard, illustrating past examples of court cases of so-called musical plagiarism. The QC prepared my affidavit. It consisted of 28 pages that began: "I, Denis King..." and was so technically detailed and profound, such as "Having used an A flat 7th chord to get over the accidentated note on 'We' on my way to the dominant ('ain't got') I get 'home' to the tonic on 'dames'..." and so on and so on that when the QC

177

handed me a pen, I said: "Sign it? I don't even understand it!"

On the 13th of June, my wife Astrid and I loaded my Clavinova keyboard into the back of our VW Golf, drove to the Strand, found a parking meter, and the two of us carried my keyboard down the street and up the steps and into the High Court of Justice, Chancery Division, where it was discovered I needed an extension cord, so, when it came time for me to perform, proceedings halted while someone in a wig scurried off to steal one from a kitchen. One couldn't help but notice that, as at a wedding, where the aisle separates the bride's guests from those of the groom, the courtroom seemed to be divided into two clear groups. The Defendant's side consisted of a solicitor representing The Pearson Partnership, the QC representing The Pearson Partnership, and me and my wife, who was just observing (and helping with the keyboard). The Claimant's side, on the other hand, was filled with grim-faced representatives from Chappell Music, Williamson Music, the Performing Rights Society, Rodgers and Hammerstein estate, and a Philip Zimet, I see by the documentation I've saved, whoever he was. They took up the entire side of the court and seemed to me to number in the hundreds. The fact that our distinguished music copyright QC's wig was slightly askew, with his black gown full of rips and a tattered hem, didn't exactly help the rumblings in my stomach, already uncomfortable from broccoli inadvertently eaten the night before. Nor did the judge's admission in his initial comments that he wasn't remotely musical.

As our QC rose to present the case for the Defence, I rose along with him and, as directed, set up my keyboard at the front of the court, in readiness for illustrating

Exhibits labelled "DK1", "DK2", "DK3" and so on. I was not allowed to speak, only play. I sat poised, listening to our QC, understanding only vaguely what he was talking about, and waiting for my cues, which were not easy to spot, even though we'd had a brief rehearsal.

"By way of example," I'd hear, "instead of playing a dull C major chord, an accompanist may choose to superadd the note B natural, thus C-E-G-B, the B clashing with the C. In practice, the dissonance is ameliorated by the fact that the intrusive B is played at the octave and is further separated from the root note C by the consonant notes E and G."

The QC would then look at me expectantly.

I'd hurriedly look down at Exhibit DK2 and hope what he was talking about was a chord of C major 7th, play it and look up, relieved to see him smile and nod to me encouragingly. In similar fashion, I illustrated, for most of the morning, what is meant by C minor, C diminished and C augmented, succession of perfect cadence, interrupted cadence, subdominant relative minor, violent harmonic transition, whatever that is, temporary modulation to Key G, and use of supertonic minor 7th D minor in place of superdominant F. I then went on to perform extracts from well-known favourites such as *Tea For Two*, *Knees Up Mother Brown*, *In A Little Spanish Town*, *The Darktown Strutters' Ball* and *God Save The Queen*, finishing my act with an in-depth musical dissection of both *There Is Nothing Like A Dame* and *You've Just Got To Meet Elaine*. It was possibly the most stressful gig I'd ever experienced since the *Bouncing Ball Boogie* at the West Hartlepool Empire in 1954 during which, as you may recall, The King Brothers had had to play and sing and bounce a rubber ball to one another all at the same time.

When the QC had finished, the judge looked round the court and said: "Before we let Mr. King stand down, does anybody have any further requests?" (which raised a few titters), I then gave a small bow to His Lordship, dismantled my keyboard, and took it back to my seat behind the QC, where my wife patted me on the arm and said: "You were wonderful, darling."

The court adjourned for lunch, Mr. and Mrs. King and their keyboard went home, thus depleting the Defence team by 50 per cent, and I heard from The Pearson Partnership solicitor a few days later. He said he didn't think it had "gone particularly well for us" as the judge had more or less implied that everything musical he'd heard in court had sounded much the same. He would not, however, be delivering his judgement for some months.

Hopes were not high, needless to say, at The Pearson Partnership, nor in the King household, as we all waited for someone who had trouble distinguishing *The Darktown Strutters' Ball* from *God Save The Queen* to decide our fate. Meanwhile, the Performing Rights Society, or PRS, the organisation which collects and distributes royalties on behalf of composers and songwriters, announced that they were freezing my television royalties from *You've Just Got To Meet Elaine* (approximately £5,000) pending the outcome of the case. I was by now not only extremely sorry I had ever met Elaine, I was beginning to wish she'd been run over by her own bus.

Despite no two notes being the same in either Richard Rodgers' tune or mine, His Lordship the Right Honourable Mr. Justice Cloth Ears decided in favour of the Claimants, largely because of the undeniable presence in *Elaine* of a hearty men's chorus, whistling, and a big brassy orchestra. The Pearson Partnership was ordered to hand over all copies of the offending commercial to the Claimants, plus the sum of £11,500. Whereupon, incredibly, The Pearson Partnership decided to sue *me*, citing my letter of indemnity absolving them of all blame in the event of copyright litigation. No more matey pub lunches and reassuring calls from their distinguished music copyright QC for *me*. I called my lawyer, John Bieber.

On the 4th of February, 1987, we took advice from counsel, after which a strong letter was fired off to The Pearson Partnership telling them what they could do with their lawsuit, the end result being that they eventually decided against taking me to court, but, as they had taken a mere seven years to decide this, it assured me of approximately 2,555 sleepless nights. All in all, what with legal costs and lost royalties, *You've Just Got To Meet Elaine* cost me in the region of £16,000, plus a sinking feeling in my stomach every time I see a National Express Rapide bus. The greatest price I paid, though, was the loss of my reputation.

As soon as *Campaign* magazine, the bible of the advertising world, published the result of the High Court case, my phone stopped ringing. The finer details of the case didn't matter, all anyone had to see were the words "plagiarism" and "infringement of copyright" and that was it, the end of my commercials career.

Two years ago, while indulging in my morning swim in the North Sea on the Suffolk coast, a woman introduced herself to me as I was towelling off. I have no idea how she recognised me, but she did, and said that years ago she'd worked for The Pearson Partnership. She said she had always felt terrible about the unforgiveable way I'd been treated over *Elaine*, but she'd been barred by the agency from speaking to me. So she wanted to do so now, as it had bothered her all these years.

"And you might be pleased to hear," she added, "that The Pearson Partnership went bankrupt, and not only that, their entire building burned down."

(It wasn't me, m'lud. Honest.)

Chapter 18

PRS, APC, and OMG

Astrid came home from the school run one day to find me perched statue-like on the stairs just inside the front door, holding a big brown envelope.

"What're you doing?" she asked.

"Waiting to be disappointed by my PRS cheque," I told her. "I can't decide if I want breakfast first."

PRS stands for Performing Rights Society and is money, royalties you get from composing. When you write a piece of music you register it with PRS, which, ever since it was founded in 1914, keeps track of what's being played where, by whom, all over the world, 24 hours a day. I have an image of little old ladies in earphones sitting at desks in wooden huts in some far off place with pencils poised, saying: "Gee, this sounds like one of Den's, have a listen, Grace."

People have to pay to play your music, be it for television or radio or in a lift or shop or even an exercise class, all of which I personally believe to be a fantastic way of working things (and allow me to say yet again how glad I am to have packed in being an extrusionist at the Lacrinoids factory in Romford years ago after just one day and to have ended up being a composer instead). On top of which, you can receive royalties for the same piece of work again and again, and a composition doesn't come out of copyright and into the public domain until 70 years after the composer's death, so my son should be okay, for a while at least.

Obviously, it's impossible to monitor everywhere every second, and if there are Pilates classes out there sneaking pelvic tilts to Denis King themes and not telling anyone, so be it, but on the whole I am very happy with the job PRS does and can't begin to imagine how one would keep track of one's compositions without it.

How the system works is four times a year a big envelope containing a computer print-out arrives in the post. Like most things, you can access it online as well but I like the envelope. I like to set it down and stare at it until I get the courage to open it. The amount is always a surprise, sometimes good, sometimes bad. The big hope, each time, is that the world can't get enough of the 52 episodes of *The Adventures of Black Beauty* (you get paid for repeats of incidental or background music as well as the theme tune) and then Astrid and I can, oh, have the shed painted or buy a new washing-machine pump or some other romantic thing, but usually I tear it open to find there's 26p coming from a song I don't even remember writing having had one play on Radio Malta. For a while I seemed to be quite popular in Chad. And, very occasionally, a title of a piece of music appears on my statement that I am fairly certain I had nothing to do with, especially as there is another composer's name next to it, but the amount is usually so small it's not worth bothering about, besides which, I tell myself, chances are that other people are receiving royalties with *my* name attached and doing nothing about it either (except perhaps buying a new Mercedes or BMW).

There is also a collection service called MCPS, now linked with PRS, which stands for Mechanical Copyright Protection Society, known in the trade as "Mechanicals". It's got something to do with the performance of the piece and has been explained to me many times, but not very well. All I know is once, instead of the £30 I'd expected, I received a whopping £8,000 for a TV series called *Smuggler* being shown in Germany, but I didn't want to call to check just in case they'd got their sums wrong.

I will now touch on a feature of royalty-accruing which, like many composers, I can, on occasion, find deeply irritating, such as every time I open my PRS statement, and it's this: if the composer doesn't own what's called "the publishing", meaning the publishing *rights* on a piece of music, the composer must *share* his royalties right down the middle with the person or company who *does* own the publishing rights. For example, for every pound I receive in royalties for *Black Beauty*, a music publishing company called Standard Music receives the same amount (or did, until I recently managed to renegotiate a modest increase in my favour) and they will continue to do so for as long as *Black Beauty* is in copyright.

When I wrote the piece back in the Seventies, it was normal practice in the world of television music to assign the publishing rights to a music publisher connected with the commissioning TV company. By signing the contract to write the music, you signed away the publishing rights as well, you had no choice, that's how it was done, especially if you were just starting out and under the impression that a music publisher was as necessary in your life as the black notes on your piano.

Music publishers, originally, way back when they were first invented, were indeed necessary in order to promote the composer's work. They published the sheet music, they got artists to perform the work, record the work, and arranged broadcasts of it on the radio and, later, TV, and the accepted split for these services was 50/50. Time passed. Technology crept in. The music world changed. Things were done differently. The question: "What exactly does a music publisher *do?*" began creeping into composers' conversations more and more because from what we could see, their job now seemed to be largely one of administration and yet they still, largely, expected – and got – 50 per cent of a composer's royalties. And still do, for the most part.

Now don't misunderstand me, this does not necessarily make them bad people, I don't much like administrative tasks myself and am happy to pay someone to do it, on top of which some of them can be quite nice, I have even on occasion allowed them round my dinner table (so long as they don't sit next to me) but generally, the whole subject of music publishing, I'm afraid, continues to rankle and probably always will.

In fact, it rankled me once so much that, carried away by what I considered the gross injustice of it all, I did something which, in retrospect, was incredibly stupid, I allowed myself to be pressured into signing a declaration compiled by equally-incensed members of the Association of Professional Composers designed to fight coercion in the world of television music. Coercion meaning that if you stood your ground and refused to let the commissioning television company publish your music, they simply hired another composer who would. We at the APC had endless meetings during which this "blackmail" seemed to be the only topic on the agenda, and a document was eventually drafted.

Briefly, although I no longer have a copy to hand, having stamped on mine then driven over, shredded, and cast it into the Thames, the document said that we composers were fed up, we wanted either to keep the publishing rights ourselves or be free to assign them elsewhere, and were really putting our foot down here, we meant business! The idea was that all 60 or so of us would sign the declaration. It would then be circulated among those television companies who were the notorious culprits, and they would start quaking in fear. Whereupon I signed the declaration, it was circulated, and I then discovered that I was only one of four composers who'd signed it, the others having been too scared to do so. At which point my name went onto a secret black list, which also was circulated, and my career as a television composer came to an abrupt end. Only then did I understand why my fellow so-called "incensed" composers, also with families to support, chose not to sign.

I became a former television composer at about the same time as I became a former commercials and jingles composer and suddenly having no work, at least the bread-and-butter kind, takes some getting used to.

The first thing I blamed for my phone not ringing with lucrative job offers was the phone itself. I came home with a new one, called a Curlew, our first cordless (supposedly rings more with TV series needing theme tunes than the normal kind) but we were disappointed right off because it only ever rang when someone else in the house was dialling out, plus Astrid discovered we couldn't use it near anything metal or it disconnected, it especially hated the living room full of brass heirlooms and the kitchen full of copper, if a call did succeed in coming in, we invariably answered by saying: "Hang on, let me take this on a decent phone!" and after going back to the store with it twice, it lived for 20 years in a corner of the attic where I threw it.

Just so we're clear. By "no work", I never meant to imply that the Richmond Golf Cup or The Wavenden Spoon, The Vardens Putter Medal, The Treasurer's Trophy Stableford, Ifield, Wentworth, Foxhills, Moor Park, Stoke Poges, Sandy Lodge, Finchley, The V.G.S., The V.C.G.S., The S.G.S., The C.A.G.A., Captain's Day or The Happy Hookers Golf Day at the Royal Mid Surrey were in any way unimportant. On the contrary, I've won, over the years, a colour TV, a glass vase, three trolleys, some silver trays to polish and screw up the phone that didn't like metal near it, and, to date, about 17,000 golf umbrellas. Astrid, sadly, though at some level undoubtedly proud of my sporting prowess, at least once she had figured out some place for the trolleys to live besides the front hall, was less than impressed from a Bringing Home The Bacon point of view, so I would periodically force myself to have what I call "another ring round".

This is where you call up all your contacts and producer friends at ad agencies and TV companies to remind them you're still alive and other humiliating info, and then find out they don't work there anymore and then become so depressed you head up to the course for a few holes.

At one point, we heard that a composer friend who worked constantly would once or twice a year send out tapes of his jingles to all the big ad agencies, and thought this sounded like a good idea, so, with Astrid's help, I recorded, labelled, addressed and sent out 75 cassettes around town. And then waited. And then not a whisper – except of course, for me saying hourly: "Isn't it strange I haven't heard back from anyone yet?"

Finally, about four months later, I got a call.

"Mr. King? This is Verity Stewart from Green, Grosse, Ploptz, Pierreponty (or Some Dumb Name Ltd.) and I've just been listening to that tape you sent?"

"Oh? Really?"

"Yes, and I notice you did the music for Rowntree's Cabana Chocolate Bar."

"Yes, that's right," I said, giving the thumbs up to Astrid across the kitchen.

"Fantastic!" said the woman. "I was wondering if you could tell me who *directed* it?"

Astrid also designed "Hi I'm Still Alive and Composing" type flyers to send to ad agencies and TV companies in the shape of partially-pre-folded paper aeroplanes, figuring, wrongly, as it happened, that all these companies would think: "Brilliant! I can shoot this right into the wastepaper basket, where it was going anyway, let's get this inventive chap on the phone!"

Plus I kept being sent computer printouts showing how badly the film version of *Privates On Parade* was doing all over the world and gross this and net that and who cares when I'm not getting a cent anyway thanks to a terrific contract where I think the man selling popcorn got paid before I did.

"Why do they keep sending these to depress me?" I'd moan.

Once every few weeks of getting no sleep I would wake up blaming my agent for no work and decide I needed a new one. Astrid said this reeked of actor behaviour, changing agents more often than your

189

underwear, and yes, I was and am aware that agents don't get you work, you get your own work, agents are for negotiating contracts and figuring out percentages and taking you to lunch, but it's better than lying awake believing it's all your fault. I had my eye on a blonde woman once (professionally), who wined and dined me, seemed nice, handled a lot of musicians, said she loved my work and promised me tons of it, the only drawback being she once used to date my brother Mike, but I decided not to hold it against her and signed a contract, whereupon she immediately got me zero work. This happened a few more times. I then lunched with a delightful agent named Patricia Macnaughton, or did until she retired, and should anyone in need of a tune be trying to reach me, am currently grabbing sandwiches with her son Rupert Lord who took over the agency, and I don't think even knows Mike.

I then thought my luck had changed when I got very friendly (again, professionally) with a big deal HBO TV producer named Lynn, having written two songs for *The Worst Witch* for her which she raved about and after she went back to the States I sent over the mountains of tapes of my music that she'd asked for, and then heard nothing. Did she get them? Did she hate them? Why do we bother? Six months later I got a long chatty letter back saying how excited she was about the real estate course she'd been taking, how it had always been a fascination of hers and how happy she was to have left show business behind. Perfect, I thought, my one sure-fire contact in the Big Apple and instead of a getting me a job she wants to sell me a house.

And then out of the blue, my luck did change, which is why, I suppose, we all stay in this quirky business. You never know what's around the corner. In my case it was a pilot for a new TV series called *Lovejoy*.

I must now take back any snide comments I've ever made in my whole life about my brother Mike, because it was through Mike and his friendship with actor Ian McShane, who starred in *Lovejoy*, that I got the job. Ian liked the theme tune I came up with, the producer Allan McKeown also liked it, and that was that, the BBC commissioned me to do the theme, and the series, which then went for a second series, and then a third, and a fourth, and 82 episodes later *Lovejoy* is still being played all over the world and I get 60 per cent of the royalties and Witzend Music gets 4 0 per cent, none of which I'm objecting to, I hasten to add, but I tell you all this so you can see it in perspective, because I was only paid the princely sum of £150 by the BBC back in 1986 to write the theme. This was not exactly the windfall I'd been looking for but the BBC said the amount was non-negotiable. Their reasoning, because you can be sure I questioned it, was something they called "standard procedure". They looked at my file, saw that I had last worked for them 18 years earlier, saw what they'd last paid me as a fledgling composer for a sitcom, and offered me the same. So my feeling is that anything that has come my way in the *Lovejoy* department since then is a bonus, whether I have to share it or not. And, though not many people know this, in fact, no one that I can think of knows this – yet – the *Lovejoy* theme is not all it seems at first hearing. Ian McShane might like this story.

Having read the pilot script for the proposed series, it was "absolutely essential", as I somewhat pretentiously explained to the producers, and Ian, that the theme itself needed to incorporate the following elements: the world of antiques, to be illustrated by the use of a harpsichord; rural Suffolk – strings and horns; and, perhaps most importantly, the lovable-rogue personality of the title character himself – a contemporary rhythmic feel.

Everyone was delighted with the end result. Certainly *I* was, because the *Lovejoy* theme was, in fact, a piece of music I'd written some years earlier for a series about a schoolteacher called *Drummonds*, which had been rejected. The old composer's adage holds true: never waste a good tune.

Chapter 19

PRIVATES ON PARADE

Out of the blue, director Michael Blakemore rang up to ask if writing the score for a new Peter Nichols "play with music" which the Royal Shakespeare Company was producing was something I'd fancy. It was about a British Army song-and-dance unit in Malaya in 1948 and called *Privates On Parade*. The composer in residence at the RSC had yet to produce any music for the show, it was about to go into rehearsal, and Messrs Blakemore and Nichols were becoming concerned. Why *I* was being asked, I don't know, Michael and I were friends, but I'd never written for the theatre before. Being the composer of *Black Beauty* opened doors, true (not necessarily ones about ageing drag queens in post war South East Asia), but whatever the reason, I was not only very interested but very flattered.

Peter had already completed the lyrics, which I thought funny and clever, and he wanted the music to be written in 1940s pastiche-style. Parody of that period came relatively easy to me as I'd grown up hearing those kinds of songs; I'd listened to Vera Lynn, Flanagan and Allen, Noël Coward, Carmen Miranda. I knew what Peter meant, and, down in my little studio at the bottom of the garden in London NW3, I found I was able to complete the score in a week, much to Peter and Michael's astonishment (and mine). Thankfully it all worked and everyone was happy.

By the time the show opened, to huge acclaim, I was so smitten by the whole ensemble experience of writing for the theatre that I never wanted to do anything else ever again, and you couldn't keep me away from the Aldwych Theatre – I'd be running in to take over as the pianist and musical director whenever the MD wanted a day off (or even when he didn't), I'd be constantly checking to see how the box office was doing, and whenever a friend or acquaintance said they'd like to see the show, practically a daily occurrence, I'd race to secure them seats, in the absurdly naïve belief that having a hit in the West End meant this was not only my duty, but that I should also pay for their tickets (which explains where most of my royalties went). It is a myth, incidentally, that we theatre folk always get "freebies". We may be able to arrange what are called "house seats", which are sort of VIP emergency seats the management holds onto until the last minute and then, if there are no other takers, sells to the public, but these we usually have to pay for, too.

Privates was blessed with a superb cast, including Denis Quilley, Joe Melia, Simon Jones and Nigel Hawthorne, whose brilliantly eccentric performance as Major Flack was so mesmerising that the band, normally a bunch of hardened musicians who pick up the newspaper or sometimes even sneak off to the pub between songs, would, to a man, remain in the pit to watch Nigel's hysterically funny scene with the young innocent Sergeant Flowers, played by Ian Gelder. At the *Evening Standard* Awards that year, *Privates On Parade* picked up many prizes, including Best Comedy. Peter Nichols in his acceptance speech thanked everyone involved in the production... except me. He apologised the following day.

Two years later, *Privates* was to have its American premiere at the Long Wharf Theatre in New Haven, Connecticut, with Jim Dale in the lead, and Peter and I were invited by director Arvin Brown to come over for the six-week rehearsal period. In the cab on the way to Heathrow, as I was making some rather astute observations about traffic volume on the A4, Peter casually mentioned that as he'd walked out the door that morning he'd told his wife, Thelma, about an affair he'd

Company shot on the set of the 1982 film, Privates On Parade. *Front row, L-R: Peter Nichols, Michael Blakemore, DK, Denis O'Brien, and George Harrison. Back row, L-R: Joe Melia, Bruce Payne, David Bamber, Denis Quilley, Gillian Gregory, John Cleese, Simon Jones, Nicola Paget, and Patrick Pearson.*

been having with a woman named Roz who lived in New York.

"Christ!" I said, appalled. "Why?"

"I thought it was only fair," Peter said, matter-of-factly checking his travel wallet.

"Fair? To whom?!"

"Thel," he said. "Oh, and I told her about the letters, too. And about you being the go-between."

Six months previously, and much against my better judgement (and despite not being thanked at the *Evening Standard* Awards), I had allowed myself to be talked into receiving letters for Peter, from this Roz, at my address in Hampstead. It was agreed that when a letter arrived, I would ring him and he'd come and collect it. The hitch was that Thelma, who I can only assume was suspicious, listened in to almost all his phone conversations, certainly his ones with me: I could always hear the click of the extension. I'd asked Peter what we should do about this. He didn't know. He clearly hadn't thought this thing through very well and I should have pulled out then and there, but didn't. I suggested a code word.

"Peter, if there's a letter here for you, what if I slip in the words 'Alistair Cooke'."

"What do you mean?"

"You know, *Letter From America*." Cooke, at the time, had a famous long-running radio show of that name. I thought I was being rather clever. After a beat, Peter's face lit up.

"Brilliant!" he said, and threw his head back and laughed.

I enjoy watching Peter laugh. It's a rather maniacal laugh, during which his head tips back, his lips part like he's showing the dentist his gums, and his upper and lower teeth fuse in a rictus-like clench. I do a reasonable impersonation of him, but only at parties.

The next time a letter arrived for him from New York, I rang Peter, heard the distinct click of the extension being lifted, and, in the middle of a discussion about a possible new song for Act Two, said, as casually as I could: "Oh, by the way. Alistair Cooke."

"What?"

I said it again.

"What do you mean?" Peter said.

I said "Alistair Cooke" for the third time, which is about as many times as one can get away with saying "Alistair Cooke" for no apparent reason, but as Peter still didn't respond, I thought it best to drop it. We continued our conversation about *Privates* and it wasn't until Peter and I ran into each other in the street some days later that I was able to remind him of this ingenious, but not particularly successful, ruse which had apparently slipped his mind.

"Of course!" he said, apologised, and came to collect his letter. I said "Alistair Cooke" on two more occasions with similar results, deeply regretting my involvement and wishing this Roz would stop writing.

By the time we arrived at the Long Wharf Theatre in Connecticut, Peter had put his extramarital love life on the back burner and we were both happily immersed in the American premiere of *Privates On Parade* until, 10 days into rehearsals, a taxi pulled up at the front of the theatre and Thelma Nichols got out.

I think it's safe to say she had not been expected, but whether she had come to stop Peter from sloping off to New York after hours or to stick a knife in his back (or mine) wasn't clear. She entered the Green Room, where we were on a break, with a face like thunder.

"Hello, Thel!" I said, with what I hoped was a cheery

wave.

"Hello, Denis," she said, sweeping past, not looking at me, and never said another word to me all week.

The tension between Thelma and Peter was palpable, but fortunately she wasn't much in evidence for the rest of the rehearsal period, appearing only at the occasional group dinner or gathering, where she kept very much to herself, was polite but distant and opted to speak only when spoken to. She did say "Thank you" to me once when I held a door open for her, but it could have been meant for director Arvin Brown who grabbed the door for her at the same time.

On the Sunday night, the night of the dress rehearsal, which Thelma attended, the cast, crew and authors all went for drinks after, in the bar of the Howard Johnson Motor Lodge next to the theatre. It was a jolly evening, the Dress had gone well, everyone was happy and Peter was showing a good amount of rictus-maniacal teeth. Arvin asked where Thelma was. Peter said she'd gone up to the room with a headache. I got to bed around midnight. At 2.45am, the phone rang.

"Denis, it's Peter! She's done it!"

"Done what?" I said, half asleep. "Who?"

"Thelma. I think she's killed herself!"

Killed herself! Christ! I sat up, scrabbling for the light switch.

"Can you come down?" Peter sounded frantic.

I threw back the covers, found my dressing gown and slippers and raced the two flights down to their room. Peter, also in a dressing gown, was at the open door, waiting.

"I don't know what to do!"

"Who've you called?" I said.

"You," he said.

"What about a doctor!" I said, pushing past. "Where is she?"

I followed Peter into the bathroom where Thelma lay in her nightdress on the floor of the shower, moaning. Clearly not dead, at least not yet. An open bottle of sleeping pills lay next to her. I rang the desk.

"Good evening, sir!" The desk clerk was full of American good cheer. "Can I help you?"

"I need a doctor! Right away!"

"I'm sorry, sir. It's Sunday night. There's no doctor in the Motor Lodge. Is there a problem?"

I said there was a lady who was very unwell in room 219. The desk clerk said not to worry, sir, he'd call the paramedics.

I relayed all this to Peter as I grabbed a flannel and ran it under the cold tap, and with flashes of Jack Lemmon attending to Shirley MacLaine in a scene from *The Apartment* going through my head, laid the flannel on Thelma's brow, called her name, tried to lift her, couldn't, shook her, patted her face, called her name again – Peter standing transfixed throughout, until I told him to go and make some black coffee (for me). There was a loud banging on the door, I opened it, two young blond husky all-American paramedics charged in and took over, and I was asked to leave.

While Thelma, accompanied by Peter, was being carted off in an ambulance to Yale New Haven Hospital to have her stomach pumped, I returned to my room and spent what was left of the night staring at the ceiling tiles, thinking poor Thelma!

And, of course, wondering how the night's events would affect the show. In a wave of unparalleled selfishness, I suddenly thought, Christ, what if they cancelled it! Would they do that? Could they do that?

199

My big break in the US of A? Sayonara Broadway. Oh dear God, dear God, I thought, please let her live! Let Thelma live!

Finally conceding that sleep was not going to happen, I got up. It was about 6.30 in the morning.

I showered, dressed, and padded wearily down to the coffee shop for an Early Bird Breakfast, where the sight of Thelma and Peter sitting in a booth chatting and laughing and tucking into bacon and eggs stopped me in my tracks. (She lived! Oh Glory! Glory!)

She not only lived, she looked up, her face brightened, and she seemed genuinely pleased to see me, which also threw me. I asked how she was. "I'm fine, dear! Fine!" she said, slathering on butter and jam, like it was the most normal thing in the world to head to HoJos for a fry-up after having your stomach pumped. "D'you want to sit down?"

I was feeling somewhat confused. They seemed so cosy with one another. Christ, had I dreamed all this? (Wait! Was Christiaan Barnard the waiter?) Assuming Mr. and Mrs. Nichols had a lot to discuss, and unable to think of anything I might contribute to the conversation other than "Alistair Cooke" or "Cor, you looked a right picture with your nightie up around your neck!", I declined their offer and found a stool at the counter. *Privates On Parade* opened on schedule with no further suicide attempts and we all went back to England.

Two years later, in 1981, at Peter's invitation, I attended the first night of his latest piece, *Passion Play*, at the Aldwych. I'd known nothing about the play beforehand, but as it progressed, aspects of the story began to look uncomfortably familiar. The play is about adultery and betrayal, about a late middle-aged professional couple whose marriage is turned upside down by a young woman who likes older men. The Peter-Thelma-Roz triangle, I suddenly realised, was unfolding on stage before my eyes.

To add to the surrealism, Peter and Thelma were seated directly in front of me in the stalls, laughing, applauding, exchanging loving glances, seeming to enjoy every single moment of the play, and I was torn between watching them or the action on stage, hardly able to wait for "my" entrance (and to see who they got to play me) and when the big moment arrived, the one where the wife finds out about her husband's affair and tries to kill herself by overdosing on sleeping pills, I sat grinning in anticipation. It took me almost to the end of the play plus much intense scrutiny of the cast list to realise that *my* character didn't exist, Peter had written me out! (Last suicide attempt I help *him* with.)

Chapter 20

MEETING 'HER INDOORS'

Following a lively first night party at producer Edgar Rosenblum's house on Wooster Street in New Haven, Connecticut, after the American premiere of *Privates On Parade* in May of 1979 at the Long Wharf Theatre, I spent an uncomfortable night in my room at Howard Johnson's Motor Lodge overlooking Interstate 95 having, as usual, eaten something that hadn't agreed with me. My plan had been to sleep late the next morning, have a wander round New Haven, perhaps see Yale University, grab a bite, and then in the evening see the show one last time before flying back to England. All of which I swiftly accomplished, as well as replenishing my swiftly-diminishing supply of Gaviscon, and purchasing the perfect "Hello I'm Back Did You Miss Me" presents for my wife and daughter, items which would be received with polite but puzzled expressions before being relegated to the back of a drawer or the Oxfam pile.

As a final farewell, the English contingent – Peter

and Thelma Nichols, Malcolm Goddard the choreographer, and I – had been invited, after the show, to
spend the night on a private island out in Long Island
Sound that belonged to actor Frank Converse and his
wife Astrid, former Long Wharf prop girl and friend of the
Nicholses. Belden Island was a quarter-of- a-mile off the
coast of Stony Creek, Connecticut, about a 20 minute
drive from the theatre, and was, by all accounts,
spectacular. Throughout rehearsals, we'd been regaled
by tales of island life by anyone who'd been out there,
heard what a magical experience it was waking up in the
morning seeing water out of every window, and we were
all looking forward to the adventure – this despite the fact
that I'm not a seasoned sailor and once fell out of a swan-
shaped pedalo on a boating lake in Upminster.

The Nicholses' plans then changed, Peter suddenly
had to be in New York the next day, so they drove into
the city directly after the curtain came down, and
Malcolm the choreographer went with them. I assumed
the midnight boat trip was off (and was in truth slightly
relieved).

"Off? Of course it's not off!" Astrid said, revving the
engine of her Honda Accord and throwing open the
door. "I've got a car-full of breakfast stuff here! What is
it with you Brits? Come on! You'll love it!"

I hesitated. I knew Astrid's husband was away filming
in Florida (and was six foot two and built by the same
firm that did the Pyramids).

"Are you quite sure Frank won't, er, mind?"

Astrid assured me that as they had constant visitors
coming and going at all hours, nobody would think
anything of it – but if it made *me* feel more comfortable,
she said, we could keep a low profile – something that
proved relatively easy to achieve, as the fog, already in

evidence before we left I-95, worsened as we turned down towards Stony Creek, and by the time we pulled up at the town dock there was little to recommend a sea voyage of any description since you couldn't see your hand in front of your face. Astrid shut off the ignition and opened her door. I took stock of the grey blanket surrounding us.

"This is where we get out?"

Astrid shot me a smile. "It'll clear in a minute, trust me." It was the last clear view I had of her for the next three hours.

Hanging onto the strap of her shoulder bag, I was led across the road and down to the gently bobbing floats where, having finally located the right "slip", I was then helped down into the *Gloria Mundi* (as in "Sic Transit...", Astrid explained), a 14-foot wooden lobster scow. Originally an open boat, she and her husband had added three low windscreen-like sides with windows at the front, and over this a canvas roof, thus creating what they jokingly called The Belvedere Lounge, and into which I was promptly stowed upon a bench and told to stay there.

Astrid – or rather, a grey blob responding to her name – leapt to and fro in preparation to cast off. To pilot the *Gloria M*, the blob explained, you either positioned yourself at the steering wheel, situated midway down the right side (which many of you may recognise as being the "starboard" side), just in front of where the canvas top started, and there you either steered standing proud, head to the wind, peering over the top of the canvas and getting soaked and blown to bits, or you did it her way, which was to bend double over the wheel, head pushed into the Belvedere to protect hair and make-up as necessary, with bottom half thrust out into the elements. Astrid announced that on this particular voyage, however, she would stay upright to afford better vision, a wise decision with which I nervously concurred.

The *Gloria M*'s 35-horsepower outboard motor roared into life and away we went, me valiantly singing the opening few bars from *Oklahoma*, which begins "There's a bright golden haze on the meadow!", then stuck my head out from under the canvas flap.

"Sorry to interrupt," I shouted over the engine noise, "but how in God's name do you know where you're going?"

"Worried? Don't be," she shouted back. "I'm used to this. Honest." I asked, with some trepidation, if there was anything she'd like me to do. She told me to sit tight and enjoy the sights, then returned her attention to the helm.

I sat on my bench for a few minutes, ramrod straight, feet together, hands on either side, gripping the wooden slats – white knuckles beginning to glow in the gloom – then stuck my head out of the flap again.

"Still here!" Astrid shouted gaily.

"Awfully sorry to trouble you again," I shouted, "but how long did you say the journey took?"

"On a good day? Oh, five minutes? It might take a touch longer tonight, though."

An hour-and-a-half later we arrived back at the Stony Creek town dock for the third time. Picture the *Gloria M* as the dotted line on a cartoon pirate map, heading nowhere near X Marks The Spot but making very pretty loops and curlicues.

"Hmm. The problem," Astrid said, as I joined her next to the wheel, "is there's two routes, the low-tide route and the high-tide route. And the low-tide route, which is the one we've been taking, not very successfully, is starting to make me nervous because we really don't want to get into the channel."

"I see. Is that… bad?"

"Yes. Because if I miss the red nun and count wrong, we're onto the big rocks by Wheeler Island. And then, you know, we're dead."

"Right." Swallowing hard, I then asked tentatively, "What about the, um, other route?"

"The high-tide route?"

"Yes."

Astrid screwed up her face. "The problem," she said, "with the high-tide route, is you can only use it at high tide, and this is only a sort of medium tide and there might not be enough water. But we'll probably be okay."

She un-looped the rope from the dock and we pushed off for the fourth time. The motor roared, we spun left into pea soup and five minutes later ran aground on what I was told was a sand bar. The sudden impact had the disadvantage of causing me to lose my footing and crack my chin on the metal bar which supported the canvas cover. Astrid raced back to kill the motor and haul up the engine.

"Christ Almighty!" I cried, lunging to retrieve my Gucci briefcase from the bilge water sloshing around underfoot. "What happens now?"

"Not a lot, until we get off this thing." Astrid handed me an oar, which I held the wrong way up and she corrected. "If you can just keep us straight on the port side, that'd be wonderful. I'll push from the bow."

The *Gloria M* was too wide to row and had to be poled gondolier fashion. A cumbersome and unwieldy craft, it was like trying to manoeuvre the *Queen Mary* with a couple of toothpicks. I asked if I might remove my tie. Astrid said of course, they'd recently relaxed the dress code.

"Good God," I said, poling madly, nipping back and

forth from one side to the other and beginning to pant. "You do this every night?"

Astrid said they didn't have fog every night and that usually the trip was no sweat, not counting the odd hurricane.

"Now," she said, standing proud like a figurehead on the flat area of the bow, "all we have to do is decide if those lights over there are Pawson Point or Trap Rock."

With ever-rising panic, I swivelled to see where she was pointing. "What lights?"

"Where the fog's brighter," she said. "Look hard."

"I am. I swear."

Eventually we got the *Gloria M* into deeper water.

Using the side-canvas supports, Astrid edged back to the helm area, hopped down, tipped the motor back into the water, started it, and, taking our bearings from this so-called bright area of fog and keeping it precisely in line with her right shoulder, we skilfully went straight into a rock.

There was no visible damage – no holes, no tideline creeping up our legs – so we promptly reversed, went around it, and proceeded to hit a total of four more (or maybe it was the same one). At long last, a big black patch of fog began to grow off the starboard bow.

"Aha!" Astrid said, with some excitement. "Land!" And headed us over for a closer look. An action I shall long remember.

Straining to see, I was almost catapulted overboard when, with no warning, she yelled "Jesus H!" and put the boat into full reverse throttle in minus zero point two seconds, having come within a few feet, as she later explained, of being mowed down by a Trap Rock Gravel Company barge the size of Long Island.

"What they do," she said, helping me up, "is chain

about four or five of them together, and because they're so big and so far apart, if you're between them, say, you wouldn't necessarily know it, because you're too far away to hear the tugboat pulling the first one."

I sat down on one of the exterior benches along the port side of the *Gloria M*, breathing rather heavily by now, staring down at the floorboards, one of which Astrid shoved back into place with a clatter of plywood then stamped on until it fit.

"But the good news is," she said, "at least now we know where we are."

"Thank Christ for that."

"Unless those barges were heading out, not in..."

Ahoy, Reykjavik!

The next land mass we came to definitely was a land mass, and stationary, which was useful, but the tide was too low to get the *Gloria M* in close enough to see whether it was, indeed, Astrid's own personal land mass.

I watched as she undid one of the yellow ropes from its "cleat", tied it to the end of the other "stern" rope, looped the remaining end around her waist, rolled up her white trousers, kicked off her shoes and, I think you could say to my utter and abject horror, stepped out of the boat.

"Where are you going!" I cried, on my feet in a flash.

"Be right back," she shouted. "Don't worry. I just have to go see if this is Andrews Island. If it is, then mine'll be right over there."

She pointed left into the fog. Then changed her mind and pointed right.

"Bye!" she called. "Don't wait dinner!"

She disappeared immediately, eaten up by the swirling murk. It felt like about a month and a half before I heard the welcome sound of her bare feet slapping back through the brine.

"We're in luck!" she said, climbing back over the side. "It's Andrews all right. I recognised their dock. Well, eventually."

Less than a minute later we pulled up at the float at the end of her own dock. I wanted to lie down and kiss it. Time: 3.10am. Time elapsed since leaving the car: three hours and 40 minutes.

Astrid hooked the *Gloria M* onto its trolley line, hauled it back out like the laundry, slipped her shoes back on, grabbed her groceries, and led me and my briefcase stumbling through the dark, up the winding cobblestones to the house, also dark.

"Don't move," she said, when we got inside. I waited, in what I assumed was a kitchen, stepping backwards into what was later revealed to be a bucket of fireplace tools, unable to see a bloody thing until she snapped the light on over the sink.

"Oh." She grimaced. "You don't look too good."

She asked if she could get me something. I said no, I'd just like to sit a moment, if I may, and get off my sea legs. I then decided I wouldn't mind a rather large scotch after all, if it wasn't too much trouble, which it wasn't, and Astrid sat down on the opposite couch with a glass of wine.

"The funny smell is a llama blanket my father brought us from Peru," she said.

"Ah."

We sat for a bit more.

"Is it me," I asked, "or is it growing darker in here?"

"It's the lights," she said. "The batteries are low. I noticed it earlier." Astrid's husband, far ahead of his time, had installed a windmill to generate electricity for the island.

The room brightened again, then dimmed. The lighting continued to fluctuate as she explained that the wind must have picked up, and that if you run lights off direct current, sometimes you get them surging in accordance with the variable winds. She asked if it was giving me a headache, as sometimes this happened to them. I managed a thin smile.

Astrid got up and switched off the electric lights, then held a match under the wall sconces until I heard the pop of propane gas catching, after which the room was bathed in a soft white steady glow. All was still, no sound

Mr. and Mrs. Denis King entertain at Abdulla bin Hamad Al Khailifa's birthday celebration at the Osteria, Chelsea, 1990, providing their own rendition of My Kind of Town, Chicago Is *entitled* My Kind of Sheik, Abdulla Is.

211

except the hiss of gas. I sat, leaning forward, elbows on knees, staring into my scotch. Astrid asked what I was thinking about.

"I'm trying to decide if I need to burp," I said, stood up, pressed on my stomach, and burped, loudly, after which I begged her pardon and she found me some Pepto Bismol. I asked would she mind terribly if I closed my eyes, just for a moment, as I was feeling most odd. She insisted I go up to bed.

Once again clinging to her sleeve like a blind person, I was led up an unlit staircase and into a guest room, where the gas light had no mantle and so wasn't working.

"But there's a flashlight here if you need it," Astrid said, taking my hand. "Feel it? Right here next to the bed?"

She then helped me find the bed, said goodnight, and I have a vague recollection of roaming around at some point trying to find the bathroom, trying to remember which colour towels she'd said were mine and almost setting fire to a facecloth, trying to see by my cigarette lighter, having been unable after all to locate the torch, which I'd apparently gone to sleep clutching, and didn't find until I made the bed the next morning.

I awoke to brilliant sunshine and the sea sparkling out of every window, as promised. I tiptoed down the stairs, helped myself to a cup of weak tea, and was at the kitchen window staring over to the Trap Rock Gravel Company, eyes glued to a moving barge, when Astrid bustled in.

I declined breakfast. She asked how I was feeling and how I'd slept. I asked if seagulls were usually such noisy buggers. She said she never heard them, that she was used to them, and explained that the sharp cracks I'd thought were gunshots were just the seagulls opening the big quahog clams they find at low tide and then drop onto the rocks from a great height, over and over until the shells break and they can dig out the live bodies and eat them. Again, I declined breakfast.

Knowing I had a plane to catch, she said we should think about going. I said I'd been looking forward all night to having to get into that sodding boat again.

By now a dab hand with the tyre bumper, I helped her cast off. With the town dock actually visible, which pleased me, the *Gloria M* bounced off through the swells and less than five minutes later we pulled into Stony Creek marina.

The pier was teeming with people, many of whom I could see in the process of boarding a ferry boat. Two or three locals recognised Astrid and waved. A dapper man in skipper's hat, gold braid and sea-faring whites, flashed an ahoy-matey salute to us, and stood watching in some amusement from above, as Astrid, down on the float, scooted back and forth trying to tie us up with a rope that, as it turned out, wasn't strictly attached to the boat. I therefore began suddenly to drift away and was only rescued in the nick of time by a grappling hook I'd been yelled at to seize hold of.

Astrid hopped back into the boat and edged me under the canvas.

"Do me a favour," she said. "Could you pretend to be gay?"

"I'm sorry?"

"When you get off. It might look better." She said she hadn't expected quite so many people to be around at this early hour, that it was obvious I'd spent the night on the island, and that Captain Carter knew Frank, her husband, was away filming.

"So, if you could, I don't know, mince, or something?"

In my panic about being almost cast adrift, my first thought had been that "gay" was yet another nautical term ("grappling hook" having eluded me momentarily too).

Astrid hauled up the motor, got the *Gloria M* securely fastened to the float, removed the ignition keys, then stepped out to offer me a hand. I leapt delicately onto the float and sashayed obediently up the gangplank, almost immediately letting out a high-pitched whoop as the whole contraption bobbed violently in the wake of an outgoing Boston Whaler, and which Astrid thought a marvellous touch, she later said, but which I had to admit was completely involuntary.

Upon reaching the solid ground of the stone pier, limp-wristedly toting my briefcase, I minced my way over to Astrid's car and as I passed Captain Carter, flashed a toothy smile, winked and said: "Hello, sailor!"

We sped off to New Haven to Howard Johnson's Motor Lodge to collect my suitcase, then on to the Connecticut Limousine depot, the airport shuttle. We kissed a quick goodbye, I thanked her for her hospitality, gave her an album of my songs (which her husband later flung into the sea) and I flew back to London where my wife met me at the front door of our Hampstead home saying "I want a separation!" before I could even set down my bags.

Within the week I was installed in a flat in Belsize Park that my wife had found, she was off to Mauritius with another man, and almost one year to the day since I'd been cruising around Long Island Sound with a stunning but navigationally-impaired, "long-stemmed American beauty" (thank you, Dick Vosburgh, lyricist extraordinaire), Astrid arrived on a TWA flight from JFK –

Songwriter Bill Solly's wedding present to us, September 23, 1984.

and never left. We were married in 1984. Annie Keefe, Astrid's best friend, who had introduced us, was Matron of Honour. In my wedding speech, with a fond nod to songwriter Sammy Cahn, I said that love is indeed even lovelier the second time around. Astrid, who was catering the wedding, was in the kitchen at the time, but everybody told her about it.

Chapter 21

YO HO HO

Willis Hall and I spotted problems with *Treasure Island* virtually from the word go, the first being Long John Silver's missing leg, which dangled somewhat conspicuously past the hem of his frock coat – our star, Jack Douglas, not much caring either for the harness or, it seems, acting on one leg.

Or indeed for learning lyrics. Six months earlier we'd sent him a demo tape of Willis' and my score so that he could get to know the songs. Douglas either never listened to it, didn't bother to learn it, or couldn't learn it, I suppose we'll never know, but the net result was that by the dress rehearsal, weeks after Clive Perry, the director, had requested that the cast be "off the book", Douglas was still very much "on the book". He paraphrased lines and lyrics or simply made them up as he went along, neither of which particularly endeared him to the writers. In addition, Mr. Douglas refused to practise with his leg harness, refused to try on his costume, and for the dress

217

rehearsal sauntered around the stage in his own sports jacket and flannels, smoking his pipe. All of which would normally be considered something of a drawback on opening night (or frankly any other night) and, sure enough, as soon as Douglas made his first entrance, a young voice in the audience at the Birmingham Repertory Theatre cried out: "Look! Mummy, look! I can see Long John Silver's other foot!"

Then, there was the parrot. The previous day, at the dress rehearsal, the live parrot who was supposed to sit on Long John's shoulder started nipping at his chin (much to Willis' and my amusement), and therefore had to be caged, which meant it no longer looked quite right on his shoulder, so it was decided that Polly, or whatever its real name was, would only be carried on periodically and hung on convenient hooks. Having made not a peep during rehearsals, once caged, no matter where it was hung, it squawked incessantly, clearly having saved itself for opening night. This was aggravated by the fact that instead of saying "Pieces of eight! Pieces of eight!" on cue, which is what had landed it the part in the first place, once on stage it decided instead to scream: "Fuck off! Fuck off!" Given that the show was aimed largely at the under-10s, this unexpected feature was not immediately welcomed by the audience.

Then there was the character of "Billy Bones", responsible for delivering vast amounts of plot right at the top of the show – played by someone's brother-in-law, so you had to be polite – but his acting voice was basically a soft yawn, which made him almost completely unintelligible, especially when he got near the parrot, an action which for some reason incensed the bird, whose language then deteriorated even further. You had to strain to catch even one syllable of what the poor chap was saying let alone make any sense of it above the torrent of high-pitched expletives. On top of which, the director had the actor busy *doing things,* while delivering his crucial plot dialogue, such as sword fighting, eating, drinking or facing upstage, and all the while inexplicably dragging a large trunk back and forth across the stage, rattling it up a long flight of stairs, then along a high platform, before finally depositing it onto, as it turned out, the wrong set of spike marks (stage markings) – something which only became clear at the first scene change.

I should also mention that the set was a hugely expensive affair with specially-installed hydraulic lifts, the idea being to transform the stage into a fantastic sailing ship, the *Hispaniola*, complete with masts, rigging and sails, right before your very eyes, and this was all great – provided the actors got out of the way of the ropes and you didn't mind watching hydraulic machinery for about a year-and-a-half. The nautical transformation on opening night was scarcely an improvement on the first technical rehearsal, when Willis Hall and I had gone out for a bite to eat and, several hours later, upon our return, the stage crew was still trying to stop the *Hispaniola*'s boom from decapitating Jim Hawkins, and get her port side level with her starboard so that it didn't resemble the last moments of the *Titanic*. My personal concern, however, was the Admiral Benbow Inn.

This part of the set seemed to fly in about every six lines, with scenes shooting back and forth from inn to inn, to another inn, then to back to the Benbow, and so on. Unfortunately, one corner of the Benbow, each time, kept getting blocked by the aforementioned trunk with the treasure map which the yawn-actor would position up on the high platform on the wrong set of spike marks.

219

During rehearsals, this had happened each and every time, without fail. Throughout the Technical and into the Dress, you'd be sitting in the stalls looking at slanted windows and doorways, waiting for someone – the director, stage manager, master carpenter, anyone – to shout: "Would somebody please move that fucking trunk before I kill myself??"

But, unbelievably, no one did. And, this not being a musical or script problem, Willis and I would head out once again for a bite to eat, during which one evening I remember we discussed The Writers Role, how by the final dress rehearsal *our* job is more or less finished, how it's out of the writer's hands and there is little left for the composer to do except perhaps help disagree on the odd sound level or say who you can hear and who you can't, and how it's now all up to the director, the musical director, and the cast – so back we'd casually strolled to find all hell had broken loose, a song needing cutting here, extra bars needed there, pirates unhappy with their harmony – and we were generally greeted by a lot of: "Where the hell have *you* two been!"

But still, no one had thought to sort out the trunk problem.

On opening night, the night the critics are allowed in, Willis and I had chosen to stand at the back of the auditorium, just in case watching Our Favourite Pirate hopping up and down poop decks all night singing whatever he felt like was too much to bear and we needed to make a quick getaway. Eleven minutes into the show, the Admiral Benbow came flying in – perhaps a tad faster than in the past – but, as usual, hit the corner of the wrongly-positioned trunk. However, instead of thudding to a halt and staying put, with one side higher than the other, as usual, it began swaying, eventually colliding with another piece of scenery which had flown in simultaneously, the centre fireplace section, now loaded with noisy Benbow Inn-type set-dressing like tankards and old copper and, I'm afraid to say, the caged parrot. After a brief moment of suspense, during which we held our breath (and the exit door open), the entire centre fireplace section toppled towards the audience and, with a considerable amount of crashing and banging and flying pewter, slammed face down onto the stage in a cloud of dust, the by-now hysterical parrot ending up in the orchestra pit. At this point, Long John Silver sprinted on both legs across the stage and into the wings.

I have no idea how the rest of the show went, Willis and I spent the next two hours in the bar with the choreographer and the lighting man, holding the set designer's hand.

Chapter 22

EDNA, ALBERT, AND MAUREEN

I have studied, close up, on several occasions, the backstage metamorphosis of Barry Humphries into his alter ego, Dame Edna Everage, but still can't put my finger on the exact moment the transformation occurs. "He" is just suddenly "her". With, as far as I can tell, no warning, and woe betide the person who then continues to address Edna as Barry; it's as if you suddenly don't exist. This can be disconcerting, especially when you're his (or would it be her?) accompanist. I am still confused about Dame Edna etiquette, so, with no one here to correct me, I am going to stick very simply with "Barry", since that's how I first met him (or her).

In 1997 I was filling in for musician friend Laurie Holloway, Barry's regular piano player, for a gig in Glasgow. Barry had come round to my place in Hampstead to meet me and rehearse a few of his songs. We had a cup of tea and some biscuits, got on fine,

223

rehearsed, worked well together, and after we'd finished Barry asked to meet my wife Astrid and young son Alex. He then asked for a tour of the house. Why, I'm not sure – it was only a small but cosy three-floor maisonette – but the request took Astrid by surprise and she raced on ahead straightening cushions, scooping up newspapers, footballs, shoes, school bags and so on – feeling, she told me later, as if we'd suddenly put the place on the market. After the tour, we all chatted politely about the lovely view from our top floor. Barry's chauffeur rang to say he was running late. We gave Barry more tea, looked at the view a little more, continued to chat, served more tea, this time with cake, and continued to chat, though I'm not sure "chat" describes it. Barry is an animated, amusing and delightful story-teller and when *you* speak, listens with genuine interest (always an attractive quality in someone), and all the while regarding you with his dark, intelligent and piercing eyes which hardly ever seem to blink. There is a stillness and an intensity about him which Astrid, who can hold her own in the best of company, occasionally finds unsettling. En route back from the loo, I heard her whispering to someone on the phone: "I can't talk, I have Barry Humphries in the living room and don't know what to do with him!"

A few days after our meeting, Barry, his wife Lizzie and I met up at Heathrow and flew to Glasgow where Dame Edna was to entertain at a private party at a hotel. We did a sound rehearsal in the afternoon then went our separate ways. An hour before the show, I changed into my dress suit and went down to Barry's dressing room, someone's office that had been commandeered (shades of King Brothers 1955, nice to see some things don't change), and where I found him with his manager, his dresser and his make-up person. Barry was in a dressing gown sitting in front of a mirror, roughly halfway through hair and make-up.

"Barry? A couple of queries," I said, sliding into the chair next to him with my music in my hand.

"Yes?" he said, doing his lip liner. "How can I help?"

He answered my questions regarding his play-on (*Waltzing Matilda*) and his play-off (*Waltzing Matilda*) and I left the dressing room. I'd got halfway up to my room when I realised I'd forgotten to ask him something about the running order, so went back, by which time his wig and sparkly glasses were on and he was getting his dress zipped up.

"Barry, sorry," I said, "one more thing..." and he walked straight past me. His manager, in the corner of the room, beckoned me over quietly.

"He's 'Dame Edna' now," she whispered. "You have to address him that way or he won't acknowledge you."

I waited a moment to see if she was serious, decided she was, and turned around.

"Dame Edna?"

"Yis darling?" Barry swung round with a smile. "Problems, possum?"

Not any more, I thought. Got it. Well, sort of. Even after working with him four or five more times, I was never able to pinpoint the exact moment that this transition takes place. Is it when the wig goes on? The dress? The glasses? Or does he just do it whenever he feels like it, to keep everyone on their toes? I've never yet accompanied him when he performs as "Sir Les Patterson, Australian Cultural Attaché", so haven't had to worry about when to start calling him "Sir Les", but I'm ready, and am thinking it'll be when the teeth go in or the huge phallus goes down the trousers.

Three months after our gig in Glasgow, I was asked

to accompany Barry for a Dame Edna appearance at a convention at the Adelphi Hotel in Liverpool. The "team" all went up by train and had a quick rehearsal for lights and sound, with us "topping and tailing" numbers – just doing the beginnings and the ends of the songs so the technicians will know what's happening.

Barry, for the record, *always* knows what's happening, and by this I mean you can count on him to be completely in control of everything he does on stage and you never have to worry about covering for him, musically, ever. You can go on stage with complete confidence, which is such a bonus because it means you can sit back and enjoy the show, and this always makes things more fun.

The speeches overran at the convention in Liverpool, which meant Dame Edna went on late, which in turn meant we missed the last train back to London so the organisers of the event had to hire a car and driver for us. At around 11pm, a bright pink stretch limo, apparently the only car available, pulled up in front of the Adelphi, and Barry, his wife Lizzie, his make-up girl, and I piled in.

The interior was fitted out with hard, uncomfortable seating – upholstered but uncomfortable – a television that didn't work, an empty cocktail bar, and psychedelic neon disco lights which nobody, including the driver, could figure out how to turn off and which continued to spin and flash and pulsate during the three- and- a- half hour drive back to London. The two ladies fell asleep almost immediately, but Barry and I, while turning various shades of pink, orange, blue and vermillion, not to mention green, talked the whole way. We discussed everything – music, musicians, writing, writers, even painting, painters and poetry, which I know nothing

226

about, but Barry, like all good listeners, seemed to find what little I had to contribute to the conversation, riveting (or maybe it was a trick of the light).

At the corner of Goldhurst Road in West Hampstead, the pink stretch limo came to a halt, too long to negotiate the last turn without taking the wing mirrors off three parked cars. My last image of Barry that night was him trudging up the road, dragging his large suitcase full of Dame Edna paraphernalia behind him. The pink limo then reversed, threaded its way back to the Finchley Road, then got stuck again at the corner of Nassington Road trying to take me up Parliament Hill, and I ended up walking home, too. Ah, the heady glamour of show business.

We've worked together a number of times since and I'm always struck by two things – how effortless Barry's act seems and, secondly, the consummate artistry that creates that impression. His really is the art that conceals art. (Or, should that be hers?)

One evening in 1975 after rehearsals at the Royal Court Theatre, where I was providing some music for Albert Finney's production of Joe Orton's *Loot*, Albert asked what I thought about the idea of his making an album.

"What, reciting poetry?" I said.

"No! Singing, you idiot!"

Singing! I was intrigued. I had just sat through the National Theatre's four-and-a-half hour *Tamburlaine The Great* and even though I had eventually given up trying to understand what was happening, there was no denying that Albert's performance was extraordinary and deservedly acclaimed. However, all I knew of his singing ability was from the film musical *Scrooge*, where he was singing very much in character. I didn't know if Albert could sing as Albert. Neither did Albert, so, a few days later, we took ourselves off to Essex Studios in London and recorded six songs, with me at the piano. (Albert also played the spoons on one of them, with great skill).

We were both pleasantly surprised by the result. Albert sang in tune and he sang in time. This was enough for us to decide to take the project a step further. He then told me that he didn't want to sing well-known songs, he wanted the album to be all original material, and asked me to write with him. Six months later, having each made time between projects, we'd completed 12 songs, songs that were for the most part autobio-graphical, beginning with Albert's life growing up in Salford, Lancashire, during the war. We found that we wrote easily together. We'd shared a similar childhood and I thought his lyrics not only well-constructed but truthful. We recorded the album in a week, after which we placed it in the experienced hands of my music publisher, David Platz, who was wildly excited about the project, "Albert Finney" being a highly marketable name. Within a few weeks David rang to say he'd done a deal.

"Fantastic!" I said. "Who with?"

"Are you sitting down? Motown," David said.

"*Motown?*" I burst out laughing, as did Albert when I told him, a few minutes later. Motown! The Supremes, Stevie Wonder, The Jackson Five, Marvin Gaye, Martha And The Vandellas, Smokey Robinson and – Albert Finney?

Still, a record deal is a record deal and Motown was convinced the album would be a smash. The actor Richard Harris had just had a massive international hit with *MacArthur Park* and perhaps Motown envisaged a similar success with Mr. Finney, who knows, but it seems their UK rep had heard it, liked it, forwarded it to Motown President in Los Angeles, Barney Ales, who also liked it. Ales played it to a couple of secretaries and people from advertising and marketing, who also liked it, and so Motown promptly arranged a six-week, first-class, whistle-stop promotional tour for Albert throughout the States. Albert asked me if I would go, too. I was packed and at the door before he'd hung up the phone, and in July of 1977, Albert, his then girlfriend, actress Diana Quick, and I flew to Los Angeles, where we were met at the airport by Barney Ales and his wife in a stretch limo, this time with a fully-functional bar packed with champagne.

"Welcome! Welcome!" Barney said. "Ya happy? Ya want some Dompa Rignon?"

At the Grand Canyon in 1977 with Albert Finney and Diana Quick in week three of a six-week tour of the United States promoting Albert Finney's Album.

We sipped Barney's Dom Perignon as we headed for the Beverly Wilshire Hotel, where I was delighted to discover I'd been given my own suite. Very nice so far, I thought, very nice indeed. Mind you, I didn't have a lot to compare it to, the last tour I'd done had been as a King Brother playing Working Men's Clubs in Yorkshire mining towns.

The following morning I was collected (from my suite) and Albert and I were driven to the Motown offices to discuss his itinerary. In the middle of a discussion about *The Merv Griffin Show*, Barney Ales turned to me and asked if I'd been laid yet.

"I'm sorry?" I said, sitting up a little. Barney repeated the question. "I've been here less than 24 hours," I said, with an anxious laugh. "Give me a chance!"

Barney, not with a laugh, turned to his assistant.

"Mike? This guy's not been laid yet. See to it." The conversation returned to more pressing business, but later that day I got a call at the hotel (in my suite).

"Hi Denis, this is Mike. What're you doin' tomorrow night?"

"Er… nothing as far as I know. Why?"

"Be outside the hotel at six," Mike said, and hung up.

At six o'clock the next night, a big black Mercedes with Mike at the wheel pulled up outside the hotel. I was instructed to get in the back, which I did, where I found myself sitting next to a stunning raven-haired Mexican young woman named Cecilia who said hello and grabbed my knee. We drove to Lucy's Adobe, a well-known restaurant in Hollywood, where we – Cecilia and I, Mike and someone not his wife – met up with Barney and someone not his wife. We were all shown into a private dining room at the back and given enormous margaritas. We ate, we drank, and I have no idea what was discussed because Cecilia's hand remained on my thigh for most of the meal. As we got up to leave, Mike followed me into the men's room.

"She's yours for the evening," he said. "Don't give her any money," he added, then pointed at me meaningfully, like Sonny Corleone in *The Godfather*.

"Motown takes care of everything," he said, and slapped me on the shoulder.

"I see. Ah! Well!" I said, zipping up my flies, "that's very generous of you. How kind."

Cecilia and I were dropped off at the Beverly Wilshire and went up to my suite.

"Back een a meenit," she said, disappearing into the bathroom. I opened the fridge and got out a bottle of white wine. When I turned around to pour us a couple of drinks, there was Cecilia, stark naked.

"You like?"

I rang Motown Mike to complain, immediately.

Well, not really, but at the risk of being eligible for the Bad Sex Literary Award, I'm quitting right here. I should perhaps add that my first marriage at this stage was decidedly shaky and in all honesty I felt little or no guilt at being led astray by the stunning statuesque absolutely exquisite five foot ten St. Cecilia of Lucy's Adobe, in my suite and, PS, Viva Mehico!

Albert's first promotional appearance for *Albert Finney's Album* was on NBC's *The Tonight Show*, with comedian Alan King standing in for the regular host, Johnny Carson. Albert was charming and funny, as usual, and seemed his perfectly relaxed self while being interviewed. Then he was asked to sing, and from where I sat at the piano, fingers poised, I could see a strange but familiar light come into his eyes.

Not one of total panic, exactly, but more the look of someone who will shortly be stepping outside his comfort zone, this would not be Albert playing a part or reciting Shakespeare, this would be Albert with no character to hide behind, this would be Albert as Albert, Albert in unfamiliar territory, Albert singing. As an accompanist you learn to recognise this look, and you adjust your concentration accordingly; you crank it up to its maximum setting because obviously you want the singer to sound the best that he or she possibly can.

Albert walked over from his chair on the dais to the microphone. Behind him, Doc Severinson's band struck up, with me conducting from the piano, and the number, *What Have They Done To My Hometown?* went as rehearsed.

In other words, we got through it. No one screamed for more but it was well received, and Albert seemed much relieved when it was over. Over the next six weeks across the States, this set the pattern for every time he had to perform on TV. He never screwed up, but it never got easier for him, and even though we never talked about it, I don't think it was really his bag.

I, on the other hand, had a marvellous time. Motown may wish to make a note, however, that at the Royal Sonesta in New Orleans I did *not* get a suite.

At the end of the tour, Albert made his second appearance on *The Tonight Show*, this time with its regular host, Johnny Carson, a man who gave the impression, at least to me, of being bored out of his mind by what Albert had to say and I couldn't fail to notice that he spent each of Albert's close-ups looking at himself in a concealed monitor on his desk, adjusting his hair and tie.

But with the exception of Mr. Carson, everywhere we went, everyone wanted to meet Albert, and since

Albert graciously included me in everything, I got to meet whomever he did. Al Pacino, whom we met in New York, had been a young theatre usher during Albert's run on Broadway in the Sixties in *Luther* and now sat transfixed by Albert's every word at dinner at Sardi's one night (while I sat transfixed by Pacino). Motown kept giving us tickets to things. We saw Kris Kristofferson and Rita Coolidge in Phoenix, Alice Cooper in Philadelphia, Diana Ross in New York, and in Chicago, went backstage to see Liza Minnelli after a try-out performance of her new musical, *The Act*. When Albert walked into her dressing room, Liza threw her arms around him. Albert had given her her first film part in *Charlie Bubbles*, which he'd starred in and directed. Also in the dressing room were Martin Scorsese and Desi Arnaz Jr, with whom Liza had just ended a long affair, to take up with Scorsese, and Arnaz sat quietly sobbing in the corner. I said very little, just sat there feeling like I'd been dropped into a scene from *All About Eve*, loving every second of it, and passing Desi the occasional Kleenex.

Motown's tour, I regret to say, despite all Albert's efforts, despite the time and energy expended by the PR people, marketing departments, distributors (and Cecilia), didn't do the trick. *Albert Finney's Album* never lived up to its promise – in fact, I'm not all that sure if it even reached double figures in sales, but I am very proud to say that both our mothers liked it.

When Maureen Lipman asked me to accompany her in her new one-woman show, *Re: Joyce!*, about the life of Joyce Grenfell, I said "No" automatically, even though Maureen was a good friend. Having spent most of my early years performing, the thought of being back on

stage sitting at a piano singing and smiling had about as
much appeal as swimming in the North Sea in the dead
of winter. Which I do do now, so forget that. I simply
had no wish to go back on stage, full stop. Astrid then
went to see the out of town try-out of *Re: Joyce!* in
Farnham, in deepest Surrey.

"It's *wonderful!*" she reported back. "And so's
Maureen. It's a great piece of theatre, it would have suited
you perfectly, you should have done it!" she added,
helpfully, followed by the slightly scornful look I am
familiar with and refer to as the 'Silent Asshole', meaning
that "You *asshole!*" is merely implied, not spoken, a look
which my wife invented and one of which I am, in fact,
the sole proud recipient.

Therefore, when producer Michael Codron decided to
bring *Re: Joyce!* into the West End but was inclined to
replace the Farnham accompanist and I was asked again
– this time by both Michael and Maureen – I did not
say "No" automatically and, instead, said I would
consider it. When? they asked. They seemed quite keen for
me to do it.

The phone would ring. "Has he decided yet?"

"It's for you again!" Astrid would yell.

Apart from standing in a downpour holding a golf
umbrella over the rooftop barbecue while our
Thanksgiving turkey sizzled in the Weber, I'd never felt
quite so indispensable before, and the longer I took to
make up my mind, the more determined everyone seemed
to be to get me on board. Producer, director, Maureen, her
husband Jack, Astrid, even Steve Conroy – the electrician doing our dimmers, whom we hardly knew but who
also worked for Maureen – said I should do it. So I said
"Yes". I got a "Whoopee!" from Maureen, a hug and a
kiss from Astrid, Alex our 18-month-old waved his

rattle, and we all celebrated with Jack's homemade fishballs in the Rosenthal-Lipman kitchen.

And gradually, the more I thought about it, the more the idea of a limited run on stage with a chum sounded fun. Michael Codron had some budget issues with my costume, as you may recall, plus he was making me shave off my beard for the role – much to my mother's delight, who loathed it, and seemed more excited about seeing my chin again than my being on stage with Maureen Lipman in the West End – but what the hell, I thought, beards grow back, and the job itself wasn't terribly demanding, my role would be just to sit at the grand piano in a dinner jacket, accompany Maureen, and sing

On stage at the Vaudeville Theatre in 1990, accompanying Maureen Lipman in Re: Joyce! – *her brilliant tribute to Joyce Grenfell.*

and play various characters in Joyce Grenfell's life. A piece of cake. I could do that! Why, I'd been performing since I was six! On top of which, I'd be entertained by Maureen for two hours every night. Astrid was right. As usual. It was all going to suit me perfectly and I was going to have an absolutely fantastic time. It never for one second entered my mind that the show would be so successful, that a short run would become a long run, and that what with transfers, tours, TV, an American production and countless charity performances, 12 weeks would turn into just over three years. And that long runs can often generate big problems.

Music may come naturally to me, but acting doesn't. I like to have my words in front of me. So when Alan Strachan, the director, said he wanted it to be just me and the piano and nothing else, no music or scripts in evidence, I became a mite concerned because I seemed to have a surprising amount to say, much more than I'd anticipated – anecdotes, information about Joyce's life, snappy repartee, a word here, a word there, different accents to remember – all this on top of filling the gaps with songs or stories while Maureen went off to change outfits. Astrid got to know my lines better than I did, and I could be heard, loudly rehearsing, in the shower.

"And then in 1944 and 1945, Joyce went to 14 countries on two separate tours."

There'd follow a pause, Astrid said, during which she would hear only water and splashing, then "No, no, no... In *1943,* Joyce went to *two* countries on *14* separate... No, you pillock, get it right! Joyce went to... Oh Christ, where the bloody hell did she go!"

Astrid would stick her head in the door and yell: "Australia!"

With the exception of Maureen's opening monologue at the beginning of the second act, I was on stage at the piano in full view of the audience for the entire show. As the focus was largely on Maureen, I couldn't draw attention to myself in any way, I couldn't cough or scratch my nose or even suddenly cross my legs, it would be far too distracting. My job throughout was to give "Joyce" my undivided attention and maintain the illusion that I was seeing and or being amused by every routine or monologue for the very first time. Referring to crib notes in my shoe or having cues written on the back of my hand was out of the question. At one point I scribbled the running order of the show onto half a postcard and secreted it just inside the well of the piano where only I could see it, and this did help my confidence until, that is, it slipped down onto the strings one night and wedged itself under a hammer, creating a tinny, cowboy saloon piano effect for the rest of the act, and I had to abandon the idea.

Miraculously, and despite all signs to the contrary, I was fine for the first 10 weeks and two days of the run. I said everything right, I came in at the right time; it was a breeze. My young son Alex learned to say: "Daddy dooween Weejoyce!" and off I'd trot to the West End with almost a spring in my step. And then one night, in the middle of Act One, my mind wandered. Maureen was halfway through a monologue when I started thinking about a round of golf I had arranged for the following day at Moor Park.

The next thing I knew, there was applause, which brought me back to the Fortune Theatre, but gave me no further clues. The spotlight came up on me. Maureen looked at me expectantly. I wasn't sure whether I was supposed to play, or sing, or talk, or all three. Maureen waited. I waited. The audience most certainly waited.

From out of my mouth spilled an unintelligible cluster of words, almost as if I were speaking in tongues. Maureen raised one eyebrow, then the other. Sadly, I could enlighten her no further. She quickly ad libbed a couple of lines to get us back to where we should have been, and, though sweating copiously, I managed to pick up her cue and go into the song.

At the interval, I expected a volley from my leading lady but Maureen was far more sympathetic than I think I would have been, which was a huge relief, but from that moment on, for the next two-and-a-half years, every time the stage manager called "Beginners, please!" I sat down at the piano on stage utterly convinced that at some point during the evening I was going to screw up, and this took some, if not all of the fun out of doing the show. And as well as the constant anxiety about places and dates and whether Myra Hess playing at the National Gallery came before or after Viola Tunnard and the fur-lined boots and Joyce's inflatable air cushion from her Auntie Pauline, I had my role as an accompanist to think about.

Maureen is instinctively musical, has great timing and always knows where the first beat of the bar is, but she needs to hear exactly the same intro, exactly the same chords, exactly the same everything, note-for-note, every time, whenever she sings. Any slight variation and you're onto dangerous ground, it simply throws her. And when there is no room for improvisation, no margin for error, the pressure is on. As an accompanist you feel you're in a bit of a straitjacket.

My GP suggested I might benefit from taking beta-blockers, so I began keeping one in my dress-suit pocket, just in case. It helped. I never took it, but felt slightly better knowing it was there. I then read an advert in the

Sunday paper for transcendental meditation lessons. Astrid was sceptical. She felt I was already showing signs of what she called "actor behaviour", which included a growing preoccupation with health. Admittedly, I had become obsessed by my sinuses, specifically the clearing of them. My in-laws had sent me a small electric steam inhaler for Christmas and before leaving for the theatre I would sit at the kitchen counter leaning over it with my head under a tea towel, snorting and breathing deeply for 10 minutes or so (and apparently filling the house with "totally nauseating" Olbas Oil fumes). These inhalations I complemented by squirting organic beetroot juice up my nasal passages, a somewhat messy procedure which had to be done in the shower along with my line-learning. Astrid breezed into the bathroom one morning and screamed, thinking it was an adenoidal haemorrhage.

But it was transcendental meditation that beckoned most seductively, and I enrolled in a six-week course held somewhere just off Baker Street, a course I enjoyed, and I believe benefited from. Although looping the small sign over my office doorknob that said "Meditating! Please Do Not Disturb!" appeared to irritate Astrid on occasion, such as every time she saw it – I can still hear her explaining to young Alex in a loud voice outside my door: "No, you *can't* show Daddy your drawing darling, Daddy's *MED-I-TA-TING*" – there's no question that transcendental meditation helped my state of mind (as long as Astrid was out of the house). I can't claim that it helped me remember my lines any better, but at least I didn't get quite so worried about the possibility of forgetting them.

We gave the final performance of *Re: Joyce!* on Saturday, the 18th of March, 1995, at the Spa Theatre,

Scarborough. Why Maureen Lipman was never considered for an Olivier Award for her magnificent portrayal of Joyce Grenfell is beyond my comprehension, and one of the great mysteries of British theatrical history. Why I didn't end up curled inside a piano in a mental home is another.

Chapter 23

THE IRREPLACEABLE
DICK VOSBURGH

I don't think it's overstating things to equate making sense of the contents of Dick Vosburgh's briefcase with deciphering the Enigma code, the Rosetta Stone or, indeed, my own brother Mike's handwriting. I once had a rare glimpse inside it at the Red Lion Inn, Stockbridge, Massachusetts on July the 23rd, 2002, at 6.52pm Eastern Standard Time, when Dick opened it to look for his credit card and for the next half hour pulled out an assortment of old bus tickets, crumpled paper napkins, newsagent receipts, cake wrappers etc, all covered with illegible scrawls. To Dick, however, it was all buried treasure.

Lyrics, jokes, notes, anecdotes, one-liners, puns, a reminder to walk the dog; all would be hastily recorded on anything handy where and whenever inspiration struck, which appeared to happen about every six seconds. Incredibly, he was able to dive straight into the disaster area and come up with exactly what he was looking for (although the credit card, which one might have thought an equally important item, he could never find).

Dick's genius as a lyricist, his wit, his wonderfully off-the-wall sense of humour, not to mention his extraordinary powers of recall, his generosity, warmth and lovable eccentricities, made every collaboration of ours something to look forward to. We made a good team and I miss him, every day.

We first met in the Sixties, when asked by producer Ned Sherrin to write a song together for *That Was The Week That Was*. Born in New Jersey, Dick had come over to England in 1948 to study acting at RADA, married a fellow student and had made London his home, writing comedy material for, among others, the Two Ronnies, Tommy Cooper, Bob Hope, Dean Martin, Joan Rivers, David Frost, as well as numerous sketches and revues.

Dick was then living in a tiny house behind Sloane Square Tube station in Chelsea, where his front door opened straight into the living room – a noisy, lively, chaotic mix of bikes, pushchairs, nappies and babies. It was always my impression that he and his wife Beryl had about 15 children, but at the time I think it was only five. In order to find the peace and quiet he needed to write, Dick and his briefcase headed out every morning to his "office", otherwise known as the Circle Line.

After purchasing a one shilling Tube ticket (about 5p), he'd board a train and spend the day traveling round and round underneath London until he'd finished whatever it was he was working on.

He'd then stuff the torn napkins or magazine pages or sandwich bags he'd been scribbling on back into his briefcase, exit the train, and head home, if he could find it. Dick's sense of direction was non-existent, but

The poster for Beauty And The Beards *at the King's Head pub theatre in Islington, 2001, with Dick Vosburgh and Sarah Redmond. I had as much fun as anyone in the audience.*

243

presumably he got home at least once, since child Number Six, Amy, proves it.

Dick once suggested we grab a quick bite at the Upper Street Fish Shop, "just around the corner" he said, from the King's Head Theatre in Islington where we were rehearsing a revue of ours, and also just around the corner from where he'd lived for at least 30 years after moving from Sloane Square. We started walking. Half-an-hour later we were still walking, at which point I asked where in hell was this place that was supposed to be just around the corner. Dick paused, mid-anecdote, looked up the street, then he turned and looked the other way and scratched his head, genuinely baffled.

"Gee! Yeah. I guess we've come the wrong way. Hey! Wait!" he suddenly cried, as if a cartoon light bulb had lit up. "Is it Friday? Are you a Catholic? They always move the fish shop on a Friday!"

His navigational skills were no better behind the wheel. Due to an unfortunate misunderstanding in his youth between himself, his American army truck, and the accelerator pedal, Dick didn't drive, probably no bad thing since he couldn't follow traffic signals or read a map either. He was invariably too wrapped up in his own world of old movies, comedy routines or song lyrics to register where we were, let alone notice anything out of the window, unless of course it reminded him of an old movie, comedy routine or song lyric, in which case his in-finite repertoire of Groucho Marx one-liners, imperson-ations of W.C. Fields or Jimmy Durante – whoever he currently had "on the brain" – guaranteed a lively and entertaining car journey. Travelling back to London from Litchfield at 1.30 in the morning after a performance of our comic revue, *Sing Something Silly*, I was far too busy being entertained to notice that we were heading north instead of south and apparently had been for some time.

"Hang on a minute," I said. "Did that last sign say Stoke-on-Trent?"

"What sign? Last sign I saw was *The Sign Of The Pagan* in 1954 starring Jack Palance and Jeff Chandler!"

"I'm serious! Isn't this the M6?"

"Well, it's certainly not the Em Eye Five!"

"Christ! We've been going in the wrong direction!"

"I've been going in the wrong direction since I was knee high to Ronnie Corbett!"

"Dick, please! I'm serious!"

Eventually I took an exit and brought the VW Golf to a halt in the brightly lit car park of a by-now-closed superstore, the place deserted except for a group of youths in hooded sweatshirts throwing stones at a skip and reminding me of the opening chapter of *The Bonfire Of The Vanities*, and where I then decided *not* to stop to study a map or ask directions, and peeled out again. Dick didn't appear to be remotely concerned that we were lost (perhaps he was just used to it), he simply carried on delivering puns and one-liners until I deposited him safely at his front door in Islington.

Even though you wanted to shake him sometimes, the joy of working with Dick Vosburgh was unparalleled, and working on *A Saint She Ain't*, his sophisticated and witty pastiche of the carefree, mindless, Hollywood morale-building feel-good musicals of the 1940s was possibly the most genuine fun I've ever had writing a musical. And also playing one. We had no orchestra, only two pianos, one on either side of the stage – myself and the wonderful musician Chris Walker – and every night Chris and I would launch into the overture, never knowing what new joke might await.

Dick, in a constant effort to cram as many good jokes

as he could into an already funny script, was in the habit of trying out new lines as he thought of them. This is a practice not normally followed once a show has opened and been "frozen", as it's called, and not a practice that actors generally much care for, having gone to the trouble of memorising their lines to begin with (and don't I know it), but the cast of *Saint* was for the most part accommodating, and Dick could often be seen having a quiet word with Barry Cryer, the star of the show, just before a performance. Barry would put the new joke in (sometimes taking the other actors, waiting for their familiar cue, by surprise) and Dick would gauge the audience reaction. If it got a big laugh, he kept it in, if it didn't he tried something else. He watched the show almost every night and even attended the understudy rehearsals.

One night at the Apollo Theatre, just as Chris Walker and I were about to sit down at our pianos for the opening of the show, the company manager came racing backstage to say the curtain was being held and the auditorium cleared, due to a suspect package in the stalls. In other words, a bomb scare. Fifteen minutes later, the all-clear was sounded and the show commenced. The suspect package turned out to be Dick's briefcase which he'd set down earlier in the stalls during a rehearsal and, inexplicably, forgotten, possibly for the only time in his life.

If the joy of working with Dick Vosburgh was unparallelled, so was the joy of living with him, but in an entirely different way. I speak for myself here, not his wife or family, and the only reason I hesitate is because there were moments during our summer cohabitation in Stockbridge, Massachusetts, when a running jump off Mt. Greylock, the highest peak in the state, seemed like an attractive alternative.

Two years after its West End run ended, *A Saint She Ain't* had its US premiere at the Berkshire Theatre Festival. Dick and I were invited over to Massachusetts for the rehearsal period and given a small New England clapboard cottage to share in the quaint village of Stockbridge. On our first morning, I got up and strolled over to the Red Lion Inn for a swim and came home to find Dick standing in the middle of the kitchen in his black silk pyjamas, dressing gown and slippers, holding his briefcase.

"Greetings!" he said.

"Hi!" I said, wringing out my towel. "Everything all right?"

"Well, yes."

"You had breakfast?"

"Well, no."

"Have you had a coffee?"

"Well, no."

"How come?"

"I was waiting for you!"

I sensed that this had less to do with politeness than the fact he wouldn't recognise a kettle if it fell on his head. There may well have been studies devoted to Genius versus The Ability To Work A Toaster, but if so, I have not read any. All I do know is that for all his incomparable talents, Dick was the least practical person I have ever encountered, anywhere, and we went through this same pre-breakfast exchange every morning for a month. For lunch we bought sandwiches and took them back to the house, and on the odd occasion that I stayed to rehearse the actors during the lunch break, I think it's safe to assume that Dick ate his sandwich unaccompanied by either coffee, tea or even a glass of water. In the evenings we were either invited out or went out by ourselves. To my knowledge, Dick Vosburgh passed away without ever having experienced the thrill of boiling a kettle or pushing START on a microwave.

The Berkshires, we learned, are frequently subjected to summer thunderstorms and are prone to what Americans call "power outs", often due to a lightning strike somewhere in the mountains. The locals appear quite used to this and their homes and cottages are adequately pre-set with torches, candles, matches and kerosene lamps, just in case. At 239 Main Street, however, no such emergency supplies were on hand, at least that I could see, in the pitch black of a Berkshire night.

I was awakened by a crack of thunder that shook the house. It was a hot night, American hot, the kind of hot where you can't get your breath and there is not even a semblance of a breeze. The air conditioner appeared to have stopped, the lights didn't work, and there was a " beep beep" emanating from somewhere. My watch said 2am. I got up.

Flashes of lightning illuminated the bedroom and I used them to get my bearings, feeling my way to the landing in the upstairs hallway where, during one of the flashes, I was suddenly confronted by a bearded ghostlike apparition in black silk pajamas holding a briefcase, and nearly fell down the stairs.

"Christ!" I said. "You gave me a fright!"

Dick, in a Bela Lugosi voice, said "Your rhooms are rheady, sir, kom dis vay!"

"What's going on, what's happening?" I couldn't even tell from which direction the beeping was coming.

"Eeet ees werry dahhhrk!"

"Please, Dick, please! What're we supposed to do?"

"Well, er, gee! I don't know!"

With Dick padding behind, entertaining me with a scene from *Abbott and Costello Meet Frankenstein*, I located a torch, purely by chance, but searched in vain for a fuse box or the root cause of the beeping, which seemed to surround and, more ominously, follow us. In desperation I picked up the phone and dialled 911. The emergency services answered immediately.

"Oh, hello!" I said. "Ah. Yes. Well. Sorry to trouble you–"

"Whatsa problem?" The man sounded impatient, in that scary way Americans have of making you feel foolish for not cutting to the chase.

"We don't appear to have any electricity here."

"Yeah? So? It's a thunderstorm. Whatsaproblem?"

"Well, this'll sound odd but there's a peculiar beeping sound and the air conditioner seems to have – "

"Don't waste my time, buddy!" The man hung up on me.

Dick, in a "funny" cartoon Road-Runner voice, asked me what I thought we ought to do about the beeping, and I answered, in an unfunny normal voice, that I was going back to bed and he could please himself. The beeping noise, which turned out to be the burglar alarm, which I didn't know we had, and wouldn't have known how to turn off anyway, continued all night. I put my head under the pillow and eventually managed to get to sleep, despite the lack of air. By the time morning broke, the power in Berkshire County had been restored, the air conditioner was back on, and when I arose I was reasonably refreshed and alert enough to make Dick a cup of hot black coffee and two slices of Pepperidge Farm toast, which he proceeded to eat, gratefully, while making notes on the tablecloth, which he then stuffed into his briefcase.

The funeral of Richard Kennedy Vosburgh took place on the 27th of April, 2007, at Golders Green Crematorium in North London. The packed congregation had to smile through our tears as the coffin came down the aisle, because on it, along with a floral tribute, sat Dick's trusty old briefcase. To this day, I wonder what lost gems it might have contained (besides the American Express card he could never find).

Chapter 24

STEPPING OUT – THE MUSICAL

I'd never seen his play *Stepping Out*, but when Richard Harris asked if I'd like to work with him on a musical version, I of course said "Yes". Granted, I say "Yes" to pretty much anything that doesn't clash with the Ryder Cup on Sky Sports, but writing songs with people excites me. It's fun. I look forward to the creative process, the meeting of minds, the heady buzz of invention. The initial period of working together with a team of two or three or however many talents, all focused in the same direction, is as thrilling for me as perhaps winning the Ryder Cup. I love it, and always have a wondrous, joyous time. At least I always did before *Stepping Out – The Musical* came into my life. Even the title of the show grates. None of us liked it but no one came up with a better alternative. And perhaps that ought to have been an early clue, because what followed was a perfect illustration of what are often referred to, euphemistically, as "creative differences", but which are more aptly described in Shakespeare's words as "the purple testament of bleeding war". As everyone in the business knows, theatre is, as I say, a joyful and wondrous thing – when it all goes well. But when the creative team fall out, it can, by contrast, induce pain, suffering, and mutual destruction. However, let's go back to the beginning for a minute.

The cast of Richard's play, *Stepping Out*, is predominantly women, and I felt instinctively that we'd benefit from having a female lyricist on board. Enter the talented Mary Stewart-David, with whom I'd previously worked on a project for Alan Ayckbourn. Mary, Richard and I all toddled off to see a production of *Stepping Out* at The Mill at Sonning after which, in the car back to London, we agreed unanimously that the play could work beautifully as a musical. That moment, Saturday the 23rd of July, 1996, 10.26pm, is worth noting, as it was pretty much the first and last time the three of us agreed unanimously on anything to do with the show, with the possible exception of when to break for lunch.

By the end of our first official creative meeting at my Hampstead home, it became clear to me that Richard and Mary, though deeply respectful of one another's talents, didn't much take to each other. I'd sensed the atmosphere growing frostier by the minute, and when Mary announced she was going to leave early in order to do the school run, Richard made some barbed remark about getting priorities right. Mary snapped something back and walked out, and I thought "Uh-oh". At our next meeting the following week, coordinated with Mary's school pick-ups in mind, she at one point said something about not really enjoying writing lyrics, Richard leapt up and said something on the order of "What the fuck are we doing here then?", which was my cue to go and put the kettle on and enquire after milk and biscuits. I knew the role well, having had excellent training attempting to keep the peace between my two brothers back in my former King Brothers career. Fortunately, the three of us only had to meet up when Mary and I had completed a song and wanted to run it by Richard for his approval.

Richard's approval wasn't always easy to gauge. He had a tendency to listen po-faced to whatever I played and sang. Mary and I eventually learned to interpret: if Richard didn't say anything after I'd finished the song, it was to be assumed that it passed muster; if he queried a line of Mary's lyric and a heated argument ensued, culminating in tears and profanity and a lot of running in to put the kettle on, we were fairly certain he didn't like it. The atmosphere at our creative meetings eventually deteriorated to the point where Richard and Mary refused to speak to each other which, if memory serves, was shortly after he called her a something she preferred not to be called, beginning I believe with the letter "C" and rhyming with "blunt".

Tensions rose. Work sessions began to be conducted by telephone. My role as Skilled Mediator intensified. Conversations went something like this:

"Hello, Richard? It's Den. Mary needs two lines of dialogue changed in Scene 3 to accommodate her lyric."

"The line works. It's the lyric that doesn't. Tell Mary she can go and–"

"Hello Mary? It's Den. There might be a tiny problem. Richard doesn't quite agree with your suggestion."

And on it went. By some miracle, the three of us managed to accomplish what we set out to do and *Stepping Out – The Musical* premiered at the Theatre Royal, Plymouth, on the 8th of November, 1996; Bob

Thomson directing, Kenn Oldfield choreographing. There followed a four-week run at Leatherhead. The show was deemed a success. Producer Bill Kenwright decided to take it into the West End. We the writers celebrated by all three going out for a drink together, a rare occurrence. I went to the loo and when I came back found Richard and Mary not only speaking but sharing some joke. Whew, I thought. Finally! A team united! We've got a hit, we're heading into town, our problems are behind us! I bought another round, Richard invited us all to the South of France, nobody told anybody to fuck off, and I got my first decent night's sleep since we'd begun the collaboration. Bliss.

Enter Julia McKenzie and Tudor Davies.

Perhaps because actress Julia McKenzie had directed the original play of *Stepping Out*, Bill Kenwright wanted to now bring her on board to direct the musical for its West End transfer. We couldn't decide among ourselves whether this was a good idea or not. I didn't see why Bob Thomson, who'd done an admirable job directing, needed replacing, and I was slightly concerned by the fact that Julia was currently not speaking to Richard Harris and vice versa due, I think, to some unhelpful remark Richard had supposedly made about her age with regard to casting a TV series of his, but Bill Kenwright was insistent that her name would add weight to the production. So that was that. Richard went off to take Julia to lunch and mend the fences and after further wooing by Kenwright, Julia McKenzie came "on board" to direct the transfer.

My overall impression, however, was that she didn't really want to. She never came right out and said so, but I suspected she was only doing it as a favour. Though to whom, in retrospect, I'm not sure.

The atmosphere at the first meeting of the *new*

creative team, while not icy, was, let's say, polite – at least more polite than any meeting the old "what the fuck are we doing here team" was used to – but eyebrows shot up around the room when Julia said she intended to replace Kenn Oldfield as choreographer with someone she'd worked with before, Tudor Davies, plus wanted all new orchestrations. Oh, and to replace the entire cast.

"The entire cast," I said, after a pause, and because no one else was saying anything. "Really. Why?"

Julia explained, politely, that she wanted to come into it "fresh". She'd never seen our production, she'd said so. I wasn't certain how you could judge a production you'd never seen, and I said so. Politely.

Mary, Richard and I spent the rest of the meeting trying, in the nicest possible way, to fight for cast members, most of whom we thought perfect, and the civilised afternoon ended with the request that the three writers from now on please refrain from ever using the phrase "Ah, but when we did it in Plymouth..." again.

Auditions were held, some of them at my home. Out of a cast of 10, we, The Writers, managed to cling onto four of the original actors including the lovely and talented Liz Robertson in the central role of Mavis, who had had to re-audition, and, some weeks later, we all assembled in a church hall in Chiswick for the first rehearsal of *Stepping Out – The Musical, Take Two*. As the day unfolded, The Writers became increasingly uneasy.

Richard Harris, for example, I found out later, was worried that Julia was working from the wrong script. As she took the actors through their exits and entrances, he became more and more convinced she was using the layout of the stage set for his original play – the play she'd directed eight years earlier in other words, and not our musical version. After watching actors being asked to exit through a wall, for example, and not through a door five feet away – the ground plan of a set is always marked out in tape on the floor of a rehearsal space – Richard, unable to keep silent any longer, finally raised the matter quietly with Julia, on a break, trying to make a joke of it. Julia's reaction made it clear that she had somehow been misinformed, and the scenes were re-blocked.

Mary and I, on the other hand, were busy having our own misgivings about the opening scene. The storyline of *Stepping Out*, both the musical and the play, revolves around a group of women and one man attending a beginner's weekly tap-dancing class somewhere in the London suburbs. We, the audience, follow their progress from being hopeless dancers, most with the proverbial two left feet, to being competent enough, one year later, to wow us with their smart, polished performance at a local charity show. We share their journey and, not to sound too corny, their laughter and their tears. The opening number, *One Night A Week*, sets the scene, and is intended to illustrate the characters' varying degrees of incompetence, their inability to move in time, find the beat, face the right way and so on. After watching the opening number being set by Julia and Tudor, the new choreographer, it dawned on us that a rather slick, synchronised dance routine was taking shape. In fact, by the end of the first morning's rehearsal, the cast was looking almost as well-drilled as the Tiller Girls on *Sunday Night At The London Palladium*. Christ, I thought, if they're going to be this good already when the curtain goes up, the audience might as well all go home after it, otherwise "where's the journey"?

We, The Writers, asked about this. We were told by Julia that that's how Tudor Davies works: he wants to set the number and then "deconstruct". The rehearsal period, usually the time I enjoy most in a production, became increasingly uncomfortable and spiky, and at the end of three weeks, on the first night of *Stepping Out – The Musical*'s pre-West End tour at the Churchill Theatre in Bromley, we were still awaiting Tudor Davies's "deconstruction": the cast in the opening number was still looking like they belonged in a Busby Berkeley film. I hardly recognised the show we'd had such a sell-out success with in Plymouth. Funny lines that had always got laughs were received in stony silence; the actress playing Rose, who's supposed to be a big jolly Trinidadian, was playing her as a rather menacing South London Cockney with "attitude"; and the big "11 o'clock number" (a term for what one hopes is the show-stopping song in the second act, and which Richard and I had by now begun calling the "20 past seven number"), which had been conceived and written as a heart-wrenching trio, was now an innocuous solo. I ran out of pages on my notepad. The show simply was not working.

The audience response was muted, to say the least. The fact that Princess Diana had been killed in a car crash the day before only added to the gloom. Producer Bill Kenwright called a meeting in the theatre bar for the following afternoon, a meeting he didn't attend due to a broken foot. Had I known how the meeting was going to go, I too might have broken my foot.

It was obvious from the first minute that there were now two opposing camps in the so-called "creative team", we The Writers versus The Director and The Choreographer, a choreographer who made it very clear, certainly to me and to Richard, that he saw this division as the two experienced and brilliant exponents of "The Musical" doing their best to make something out of second-rate material provided by three dilettantes who didn't know what they were doing. In a letter to Bill Kenwright, Tudor Davies, in fact, called my music "sub-standard Sondheim", but my thinking is that to be mentioned in the same breath as The Master is not the worst insult in the world. In any event, what ought to have been a pow-wow to figure out why in hell this show wasn't working as it had done *when we did it in Plymouth* (which no one said, or maybe they did), never happened. Instead, when I (backed by Richard and Mary) insisted that the "11 o'clock number" didn't work as a solo, at all, no matter how beautifully Liz Robertson sang it, that it *had* to be re-staged as the trio in which we'd conceived it, Julia, in tears, turned on her heels and with Tudor in tow, swept into the auditorium where the cast waited for notes. The first note being to tell Liz Robertson, in front of everyone, that The Writers had decided to axe her solo, after which the rest of the cast gathered around both Julia and Liz sympathetically and from that point on tended to glare at us with a certain amount of hatred.

After two weeks at the Churchill Theatre, Bromley, *Stepping Out – The Musical* limped up to Newcastle with no further sign of Julia since the non-pow-wow meeting and hence, no one at the helm, which put me, for one, even more on edge, since the whole point of a pre-West End tour is to fix the show, to get it right, and this wasn't happening.

Re-enter Bill Kenwright With The Broken Foot. Ta Da!

Bill insisted that Julia's name on the bill was still crucial to the show's appeal in London (if it even made it that far) and somehow persuaded her to stay on board, in name only, save for a trip to Newcastle to re-stage the aforementioned "11 o'clock number" into a trio. Mary and I were already up there, hoping to give the cast, who knew the show was in tatters, a little moral support as they staggered on. Julia acknowledged me with a curt "Hello" and afterwards asked pointedly if I was happy now (yes), and we never saw her again.

Before *Stepping Out – The Musical* eventually opened at London's Albery Theatre in October 1997, producer Bill Kenwright With The Broken Foot limped in on crutches to re-stage the entire show, one could almost say single-footedly. It ran for just four short months, despite some good reviews and Julia's name on the bill. It was not a success. It didn't make any money. I didn't have a good time working on it; I don't think too many of us did. I haven't spoken to Julia McKenzie since, or she to me, which I suppose I understand. The very mention of the name Tudor Davies puts me off my dinner, and I imagine I have precisely the same effect on him. Mary, Richard and I, unbelievably, worked on another musical together, which never saw daylight, but we probably won't be rushing to closet ourselves together in my office anytime soon.

Still, I have a very nice signed and beautifully framed poster of *Stepping Out – The Musical* that Bill Kenwright gave me for opening night, which I will treasure, I'm sure, one day. In a hanging-on-the-loo-wall kind of way.

Chapter 25

THE GREAT MAN

If ever Alan Ayckbourn asks you to collaborate with him on a new musical, just say "Yes", even before you know anything about it, because whatever he turns his hand to is guaranteed to be extraordinary and the learning experience will be irreplaceable, notwithstanding the Scarborough weather and (if you are lucky enough to be his houseguest) the interminable hike up to the Stephen Joseph Theatre from Longwestgate. To be perfectly honest, even if Alan asked me to paint his kitchen I'd say "Yes". I stand in awe, all five foot five and three quarters of me, of this great man of the theatre (all six feet of him).

We first met when I went up to Scarborough with Maureen Lipman to do a week of *Re: Joyce!* as a fundraiser for Alan, who was in the process of converting the Odeon Cinema into his theatre's new home. We seemed to get on well, well enough for me to later send him a script of *Baby On Board*, a new musical I'd written with Mary

Stewart-David. Much to my surprise, he wrote back inviting us up to discuss the project – I say "surprise" not because it wasn't a good show, but because you get so used to sending out scripts to directors or producers and never hearing from them again, the exceptions here being The Three Michaels and another Alan: Blakemore, Codron, Grandage and Strachan, all of whom are prompt, pleasant and constructive. Having said that, could one of you please ring, because I wouldn't mind working with you again. (Note to Mr. Codron: I *shall* be wearing The Jacket and the rent remains the same.)

Alan Ayckbourn not only liked our musical and wanted to schedule it into his next season, but asked, almost apologetically, if Mary and I would "mind very much" if he directed it. Funnily enough, we said that would be fine.

The *Baby On Board* experience was the beginning of a friendship and a deeply pleasurable, at least for me, Ayckbourn/King working relationship that continues to this day, the finer nuances of the partnership I will now delineate for you. How it works is this: I get on with my life, that is, do other projects, swim, play golf, walk the dog, see what's for dinner, plus check my inbox twice an hour to see if there's an email from Sir A asking if I'd like to collaborate on some exciting new musical project and, every three or four years, I'm delighted to report, there seems to be one, at which time I push PRINT and go racing down the stairs with it.

"Alan wants to do another musical!" I tell my wife, Astrid, often to be found in the kitchen.

"Really? Good. Why do you keep putting the colander in with the baking trays?" she says, to which there is no answer other than that I'm a complete idiot. But at least an idiot that Alan wants to work with.

Initially, the Ayckbourn/King Creative Process worked thusly:

Alan would come up with the idea and we would briefly discuss it. A synopsis or sometimes even the completed script would arrive in the post. I would read it, tell Astrid how good it was, she would read it, agree, I would give Alan my musical thoughts, and soon a lyric would arrive from Scarborough by fax. I would set Alan's lyric to music, record it, and send him the tape of it. Later, with the advent of computers and music software, I would email him the song, which Alan would download, listen to, make minor adjustments to if necessary, and our song would travel back and forth until we were happy with it. We would complete the entire score in this fashion, usually in about two weeks, perhaps less.

During our first collaboration, a Christmas revue for the Stephen Joseph Theatre called *Cheap And Cheerful*, I had reservations about one of Alan's lyrics. It had a slightly imperfect rhyme, and, like two of my late collaborators, Benny Green and Dick Vosburgh, I am saddled with a wholly incurable aversion to slightly imperfect rhymes. However, I had even greater reservations, as you may imagine, about saying this to The Great Man; I didn't quite know how to broach it but at the same time was incapable of letting it go. After a week of her sleep being interrupted by my tossing and turning, Astrid said "Oh for Chrissakes, stop fussing. If it bugs you, tell him! And turn off the light!"

Which I did. And, next day, over the phone – in itself a triumph because Alan loathes using the phone – I told him. To my (immense) relief, he was fine about it, readily agreed the rhyme didn't work, and within 10 minutes had faxed me four alternative versions, all of which were spot-on perfect.

Two years after that, we created a musical full of perfect rhymes called *Whenever* for the Stephen Joseph, a pleasurable experience only slightly spoiled by the news at breakfast one morning during rehearsals that George W. Bush had been elected the new US President, which put both of us off our corn flakes – and then in February 2002, having been commissioned by the National Youth Music Theatre, we started work at our customary breakneck pace on *Orvin – Champion Of Champions*.

With Alan in Scarborough and me in London, the score was completed by the beginning of April, after which the show was put on hold until the following year when auditions were held both regionally and in London. Alan came down from Yorkshire and over two weekends at the Oval House in Kennington we saw more than 400 aspiring young actors, eventually arriving at a cast of 40. It's always hard to choose, when there's so many, and the selection process this time was complicated by the fact that the National Youth Music Theatre was auditioning for three of its other shows at the same time on the same premises, and because they didn't want the kids to know which show was which in case they all raced to audition only for the Ayckbourn (and King!) opus, the NYMT gave each of the four production teams a code name. For some reason the theme was oriental fruits.

Alan and I were "The Lychees", which we found amusing, although not quite as amusing as the 20-foot giant pink phallus on the set where we were auditioning. We were reliably informed that this was for a new gay revue. The National Youth Music Theatre was in a bit of an uproar trying to work out ways of disguising it so that all these hundreds of youngsters auditioning for

"Mango", "Kiwi", "Lychee" and so on didn't have to stand next to it or, worse, go home and tell their mothers.

Alan's and my disguise suggestions, for the record, included hat, gloves and possibly sunglasses. What a great business this is.

One evening, having by this time worked on four musicals together, Alan confessed to me that he doesn't really like musicals. I said nothing for a few seconds, trying to make sense of this (somewhat alarming) news, then decided to make him explain himself, because I know he likes music, indeed listens to it in almost every free moment, I would even call it a great passion. I only got as far as "But, Alan – " when, in the next breath, he put forward an idea for his final production as Artistic Director at the Stephen Joseph Theatre, and the idea was to write (yes!) a musical, and to write it with me, so I let the matter drop and haven't brought it up since.

Alan's brief was that he wanted us to write "a musical without musicians".

"Ah," I nodded sagely, having absolutely no idea what he was talking about. He cited a Honda ad on TV where all the sound effects were made by human voices. I knew the ad, and was further excited by the suggestion that we go away with our wives to somewhere hot and sunny with a swimming pool and write the show, rather like collaborators do in the movies, a sort of working holiday. This turned out to be two weeks at a staggeringly expensive rented villa overlooking St. Tropez bay.

The place indeed came with a pool but no piano. This was soon found for us, along with some loo paper. Neither did it have any place to put soap in the master shower, so Astrid and Heather, Lady Ayckbourn, spent our first evening in France manufacturing a holder out of a Tupperware container and some old lengths of twine they'd found in the basement. Being new to renting villas in the South of France, I found it all wonderful and absolutely fantastic. I had envisaged, even before we got there, a couple of hours' graft at the piano in the morning and the rest of the day stretched out on a sunbed by the pool or off somewhere très chic sampling the local wine.

"Where are you going?" Alan said, on the first afternoon. I stopped, and looked into the little room off the hall where he was seated in front of his laptop.

Alan Ayckbourn and I pause for lunch during rehearsals for Awaking Beauty *at the Stephen Joseph Theatre in Scarborough in 2008 – Alan's final year as Artistic Director. I don't know what we're looking at. Maybe someone else's plate.*

"Thought I might take a dip!" I said, with some enthusiasm. I'd been hammering away at the piano in the dining room all morning. We'd written two songs. We'd only been there a day.

"We're here to work you know," Alan said, with a smile, Alan Who Apparently Likes To Work More Than I Do.

"Of course we are!" I smiled, then hesitated between the pool or the dining room. Eventually I compromised and opted for the kitchen, where I made myself a coffee, but by Day Three, I had it figured out. After a surreptitious and apparently innocent check to see that Alan was buried in his computer with his headphones on, I'd tiptoe past his open door, swimsuit under my clothes, and make a beeline for the pool, where I'd take a brisk but refreshing swim, say a quick hello to the sun, then scurry back to my post in the dining room, towelling madly, and if Alan noticed the wet footprints leading to the piano four times a day he never said anything. By the end of our two-week "holiday", I had been to the shops exactly once (for Gaviscon and dental floss), out to dinner three times, helped demolish a case or two of local wine, used every towel in the place, and Alan and I had completed the score of what was to become *Awaking Beauty* – a musical that Alan describes as an adult fairy tale, a sequel to *Sleeping Beauty*.

On our final night, after a celebratory bottle of champagne and some excellent calves' liver Veneziana, Alan and I played through the entire score of the show for Astrid and Heather – me singing and Alan narrating – with our two ladies ensconced on the steps leading down into the dining room, eyes bright and attentive, raising glasses of local rosé and clapping with delight as required (and as they have of course been trained to do).

Awaking Beauty opened at the Stephen Joseph Theatre in Scarborough on the 16th of December, 2008. The first night of Alan's last show as Artistic Director. The challenge for me as the composer, having written the songs, had been to orchestrate the accompaniment without using musical instruments, with the exception of a keyboard, only voices. We had a cast of 10, all with outstanding voices, and the end result was not only electrifying, for me, but immensely satisfying. Alan is a true man of the theatre. I feel fortunate to have met him, worked with him, enjoyed his company and generosity, stayed in his house and, of course, swum in his indoor heated pool. And now if you'll excuse me, I must just pop upstairs and check my email.

Chapter 26

PUTTING DOTS ON PAPER

Having by now composed more than 30 stage musicals of which 23 were produced with varying degrees of success, I feel qualified to make the following statements with regard to writing for the musical theatre:

RULE NUMBER 1: A good collaboration is essential

By good, I mean finding a partner or partners whose work you respect. It helps if you like them, too, obviously, then it's more fun and something you can look forward to. I'm thinking now of all the book writers and lyricists I've worked with and can say without hesitation that I would drop everything this second to write with Benny Green or Dick Vosburgh again, Keith Waterhouse and Willis Hall, Myles Rudge – but they're all gone. Of course, Alan Ayckbourn's still very much alive, which is nice, as is Mary Stewart-David, but I honestly think Alan's happier writing plays and Mary's well, I don't know what Mary's happier doing. There's Don Black, with whom I always enjoyed working but he's constantly busy. Richard Harris, he's still around, and as it happens, has come up with a project which we may even finish before one of us snuffs it, which would be good news.

And then there's Peter Nichols, with whom I wrote *Privates On Parade* but who I'm not sure where precisely to place in my line-up of favourites, because it's a tricky one. I most certainly respect Peter's work and I do like him, and my entrée into writing for the theatre was after all entirely thanks to him, but all these years later I can still be occasionally niggled, in fact imagine my top lip ever so slightly curled as I speak, by what has come to be known in my family as *The Poppy Experience*.

After our success with *Privates On Parade* in 1977, Peter suggested we meet and discuss a project which had taken his fancy, a musical about the Opium Wars, to be done in pantomime style, and called *Poppy*. We met, discussed it, he wrote some lyrics, I wrote some tunes, Philip Headley at Stratford East was keen to produce, and we happily proceeded with the score until, a few weeks later, Peter rang to say that Terry Hands, then co-Artistic Director with Trevor Nunn at the Royal Shakespeare Company, had heard about *Poppy* and was "very interested", specifically with a view to launching the grand opening of the New Barbican Theatre with it. Peter, possibly sniffing a better offer, asked me what I thought, I said it sounded, well, exciting! Terry Hands asked for a cassette of our yet-to-be-completed score, so I went into a studio, recorded the songs, and sent them to him. Within a week a letter arrived back.

"Thank you for your effort. It was very interesting,

but we have not as yet decided who the composer shall be." It said. I could see that Terry Hands had sent a copy of the letter to Peter as well.

I rang Peter.

"Typical RSC!" he said. "Don't take any notice of it!"

"Quite right," I replied and wrote back to Terry Hands pointing out: a) his mistake; and b) that I most certainly was the composer of *Poppy*. Terry Hands wrote back once again saying they hadn't yet chosen the composer but that in any case, he felt my music was "too laid back", "too bar-room piano" and "not pungent enough". I happen to have committed those exquisite phrases to memory, no need to refer to notes.

I rang Peter. He was in the Dordogne and unreachable. I looked up "pungent" in the dictionary. Maybe my tunes weren't "smelling strongly" enough but other things were certainly starting to, especially when, while talking to my agent Roger Hancock about another matter, I learned that Peter had already signed a contract with the RSC for *Poppy* – but for his book and lyrics only, no mention of the music.

A postcard arrived from the Dordogne, followed by a two-page letter in which Peter wrote that he was sorry things hadn't worked out but, on reflection, he had to agree with Hands about my music not being right after all. The next I heard was that the James Bond composer Monty Norman had been commissioned to collaborate with Peter on the score. Terry Hands explained that he and Trevor Nunn and the RSC had been looking for a "Monty Norman vehicle" for a while and this fitted the bill.

Poppy opened at the Barbican in the autumn of 1982 and Astrid and I were dragged to see it by director Michael Blakemore and his then wife, designer Tanya McCallin. It was hard, I grant you, to be objective in my rejected state of mind, but I don't honestly think the production worked. Monty Norman's music, however, seemed adequately pungent and Astrid was caught humming it only once.

As for Peter, with whom I soon thereafter had to collaborate closely on the film version of *Privates On Parade*, I managed, just about, to refrain from impaling him on a passing fixed bayonet, but to this day, I've continued to find his conduct in all of this very odd indeed, in that he has acted as though I had had no involvement whatsoever in *Poppy*. Has he forgotten? I think if *I* were in his shoes I'd tend to avoid a sore subject, but he not only mentions the show, he often talks at length about what a disappointment it was to him. This is the man, remember, who when accepting the Best Play Award for *Passion Play*, condemned in his speech the appalling lack of loyalty in the theatre.

I use the phrase "to this day" advisedly, because 30-odd years on, as I was putting the finishing touches to these memoirs, I stumbled across a rather alarming piece of information. The distinguished theatre academic Dr. Alec Patton wrote his 2007 thesis on Peter Nichols, which was subsequently published and which very recently I was fortunate enough (if that's the word) to read. In it, Dr. Patton often quotes directly from Peter's letters, and in a particularly pungent discussion about *Poppy* he reveals that the request to replace me as composer on the show came *not* in fact from the RSC, but from Peter himself. I quote:

"And before the production could proceed any further, Nichols had a favour to ask of Terry Hands: he needed to get a composer fired. Nichols was trying to fire King (who was a good friend) without the order appearing to come from him. Hands understood what Nichols wanted from him, and carried it out elegantly."

Well, I wouldn't go *that* far.

But hey, forgive and forget, I say. ("Too laid back"? Too "bar-room piano"? "Not pungent enough"? Cloth-eared cretins.)

RULE NUMBER 2: Have faith in your own judgement; don't let the bastards screw things up

Absolutely the only advantage in bowing to the advice of people you don't respect is that when the show closes overnight or disappears without a trace, you can blame them.

RULE NUMBER 3: Prepare yourself for criticism

The only difficulty here is that there's no comfortable way to do this, at least I haven't found one. Criticism, whether it's from the press, friends, family or even the postman, stings. Sometimes, on the other hand, it just niggles or makes no sense at all. When *Lost Empires*, a musical adaptation of J.B. Priestley's book by Willis Hall and Keith Waterhouse, opened in Darlington, I received this notice, in the one review which even mentioned there was actually music in this musical:

"Denis King's music is handy."

Handy? What in hell does that even mean? As in, wasn't it lucky I just happened to have a song called *Twice Nightly* rolled up in my back pocket when, ambling through the streets of London one evening I heard someone wailing from an open window: "Oh if only we had an opening song for Act Two, but where to find one this time of night??"

And then at other times it does more than sting; it rips

apart your whole being. Even a headline can do that. Benny Green and I once wrote a musical called *Valentine's Day* based on Shaw's *You Never Can Tell*, which opened to unanimously bad reviews. These were then referred to in a memorable *Evening Standard* headline which read "Valentine's Day Massacre!", something which affected my digestion for months. In fact, if I read the reviews again, which I unfortunately just have, I find myself scrambling anew for the Gaviscon and even pondering the virtues of gastric surgery.

A bad review also has the power to affect not just you personally, but can singlehandedly determine the future of a show, particularly in America.

A Saint She Ain't, the Hollywood movie musical pastiche I wrote with Dick Vosburgh, had a roaring success when it opened at the King's Head Theatre in Islington, packed houses, and the kind of reviews you dream about. *Saint* then transferred to the West End, where it again received wonderful reviews before being picked up by the Westport Country Playhouse, a prestigious theatre in Connecticut run by the then Artistic Directors Anne Keefe and Joanne Woodward. The preview audiences adored it and were on their feet nightly which, in fact, isn't saying much since Americans seem to get on their feet for anything, but take it that we had a potential "hit". The signs were there. There was a buzz. There was that sweet smell in the air. Producers from New York were ringing up for tickets, Paul Newman said hello to me and let me use his pool; it was an exciting time. Then a review came out in *Variety*, the American showbiz bible, tearing the production to pieces. The critic, Markland Taylor, hated everything about the show. It was based on a not particularly good preview he'd seen at the Berkshire Playhouse three weeks earlier in

Massachusetts but so what, such is the power of one man and one newspaper that overnight all the New York producers and potential publishers cancelled their tickets and *Saint*, sadly, hasn't been done since.

(A few months after we got back from the States, Dick Vosburgh rang up. "Greetings! Good news!" he cried, his voice jubilant. "Markland Taylor's dead!")

Writers, I think it's safe to say, don't want criticism, ever, and certainly when it's not asked for and especially not when your show is up and running and there's no way of changing anything even if you wanted to. No one sums this up better than Stephen Sondheim.

"*Nobody cares what you think,*" he informed a naïve Jason Robert Brown, now an award-winning Broadway composer. The young man had just seen a Sondheim musical and made the mistake over dinner afterwards of imagining that Sondheim was interested in hearing his critique. He very quickly realised his error, and rang Sondheim the following day to apologise. This, in Brown's words, is what Sondheim told him:

"Once a creation has been put into the world, you have only one responsibility to its creator: be supportive. Support is not about showing how clever you are, how observant of some flaw, how incisive in your criticism. There are other people whose job it is to guide the creation, to make it work, to make it live; either they did their job or they didn't. But that is not your problem. If you come to my show and you see me afterwards, say only this: 'I loved it'. It doesn't matter if that's what you really felt. What I need at that moment is to know that you care enough about me and the work I do to tell me that you loved it, not 'in spite of its flaws', not 'even though everyone else seems to have a problem with it',

275

*but simply, plainly, 'I loved it.' If you can't say that,
don't come backstage, don't find me in the lobby, don't
lean over the pit to see me. Just go home, and either
write me a nice email or don't. Say all the catty, bitchy
things you want to your friend, your neighbor, the
Internet. Maybe next week, maybe next year, maybe
someday down the line, I'll be ready to hear what you
have to say, but at that moment, that face-to-face
moment after I have unveiled some part of my soul,
however small, to you, that is the most vulnerable
moment in any artist's life. If I beg you, plead with you
to tell me what you really thought, what you actually,
honestly, totally believed, then you must tell me 'I loved
it'. That moment must be respected."*

Unfortunately, I have yet to see these momentous
words printed in large type on any theatre programme but
they should be, because people never tire of telling you
what they think is wrong with your show. Their house
might have just burned down, their daughter might be
getting married the next day, they might have only three
hours to live, but somehow they find the time to voice
their opinion on your work, never for one second
dreaming you don't want it or need it or that that
bemused look on your face comes only from picturing
the person being slowly lowered, screaming, into a pit full
of vipers.

The postman I can forgive (almost); it's not his field,
besides which the next day I can criticise the way he jams
catalogues through the letterbox, but when criticism
comes from family, as it invariably does, or people in the
business, people who *should know better*, it's another
story. Something strange happens to normally bright,
intelligent people the minute they come backstage to say

276

hello after a show: they leave their brains at the stage door. For this reason, my lovely wife Astrid, who has spent many years welcoming visitors into dressing rooms, first her mother's, then her first husband's, then mine, has thoughtfully compiled a set of guidelines for those well-wishing audience members flocking backstage and hoping to find themselves welcome. I include them for you here, because I like them:

A: There is no such thing as too much praise. Dish it out like there's no tomorrow, even if it was the worst show you've ever seen and you spent the night looking at your watch thinking "I could be home watching old reruns of The Waltons.*"*

B: Dish out praise evenly. If there's more than one actor or writer in the dressing room you've poked your head into, don't tell one how terrific he is without telling the other. It could lead to fights on the playground later.

C: Don't say "Fantastic set!" or "Loved the costumes!" to people who have nothing to do with sets or costumes, such as the star or playwright. Everyone knows that "Loved the set!" is code for "Hated the show!"

D: Never joke with the writer, saying "It's all right, I've sorted out the ending for you!" and don't tell the composer that one of his songs reminded you of Get Me To The Church On Time *even if it did. In fact, even humming* Get Me To The Church On Time *on the way to dinner after will do nothing for the relationship (or marriage).*

E: Unless specifically asked or unless there is some anecdote connected to it which has a direct bearing on the show and how brilliant it is, do not discuss your route to the theatre. The first thing out of your mouth should not be "Del didn't want to drive so we took the Tube and changed at Liverpool Street". Nor should you walk in saying "Aren't there a lot of stairs in this theatre!" or say, as actor Michael Gambon's mother once did, "Have you any idea where I can buy linen sheets in this area?" Nor should you begin carefully describing the smoked salmon parfait you had for lunch.

F: You can sometimes get away with standing like a lemon in the dressing room doorway saying nothing, but only if you're a non-showbiz type such as neighbour, school-run parent, electrician who did the upstairs wiring etc. and overcome by being backstage for the first time. If anyone says "Did you enjoy the show?", nod. If you're offered champagne, accept it. If for whatever reason you felt like saying "HUGE thanks for arranging (not to mention paying for) our tickets!" it would be completely appropriate.

G: Deliberately ambiguous remarks such as "You!", accompanied by an awed shake of the head, or "You've done it again!", or "Good was not the word!", or "Your performance was Titanic!" or "What you did out there tonight..." and letting your voice drift off, should all be accompanied by a meaningful hug. The actor will not in any case be listening, and will in fact be looking to see who just came in.

H: Ideally, parents should not be allowed backstage without first being sent through screening devices like at airports, to catch any comments that make offspring want to hurl themselves off Waterloo Bridge with stage weights tied to their ankles. These include "Your bust looked like two watermelons", "That bald patch on the back of your head sure catches the light", "You weren't bad, all things considered", "I nearly broke my neck on the way to the gents during the first act" and "I'll tell you who was wonderful, that lovely little red-haired gal playing your maid". The correct and only line for parents is: "Well done, I'm so proud of you, you make me very, very happy". And, should you by any chance have teenagers or toddlers in tow likely to contradict everything coming out of your mouth or reveal how many times you yawned, leave them outside tied to the railing or as you go in, ask the stage doorman for some gaffer's tape.

RULE NUMBER 4: Writing musicals is not always the infallible Get Rich Quick Scheme it might appear

You want it to be, of course, and always hope it might be, but as screenwriter William Goldman once said about show business, "Nobody knows anything". And it's true. You're given a million excuses by producers as to why a show hasn't worked: too expensive, not enough of a star name, lack of tourists, theatre too big, theatre too small, the weather, the season, terrorists, volcanic ash from Iceland, and you might well sigh and grudgingly accept their explanations but inside you want to curl up and die. When your show fails, "it's a catasta-stroke", as Dick Vosburgh wrote in *A Saint She Ain't*, a whole chunk of your life has been erased, something that *was* your life, for so long, is now suddenly gone, fizzled. I once had five musicals produced in the space of a year. I thought the odds were in my favour. My plan was to be a millionaire by the age of 50. Later I upped it to 55. Now I'm hoping for £2.10 by next Friday.

The thing is, though, you have to keep going, never stop writing. Keep at it, do your best, believe in your ability, and if your show gets on, great, but if it closes without being translated into 50 languages despite your mother liking it a lot, well, on to the next. I am grateful to at least have had the opportunity to do what I love doing, which is writing songs and hearing them performed. My wife feels this to be a "very grown-up attitude".

"But darling heart," I tell her, "what would you have me do? Sit around sobbing?"

"Always works for me," she says.

RULE NUMBER 5: Few things get you out of a funk and onto the golf course playing like a demon faster than reading a scathing review of someone else's work, especially a friend's

Savour it, and keep it in your locker.

Substantial royalties can be earned from repeats.

CODA

Dr. Johnson may have said "When a man is tired of London, he is tired of life; for there is in London all that life can afford" but I've not found this to be the case. Having lived all my life there, I was starting to find almost every aspect of London tiring. The traffic, the fumes, the price of a simple cup of coffee.

Advances in music technology meant I no longer needed physically to be there. I began to dream of a place called "the country", somewhere I'd never lived but wanted to try. Astrid, who sided completely with Dr. Johnson, assured me that the likes of lawn mowing or cleaning gutters or trimming hedges weren't remotely up my tree-lined alley, but thanks to my powerful powers of persuasion, it took me a mere 10 years to get her to come round to the idea. She now says it's because she looked at me one day and saw a tired, old-ish man with a grey beard for whom the fun seemed to have gone out of life, and so figured she'd better say "Okay! Fine! Let's try it!" before I started reading up on Virginia Woolf while measuring the depth of Highgate Pond.

In January of 2005 we sold our house on Parliament

Hill in Hampstead and moved north east to the Suffolk coast. We rented, at first, a converted barn. Astrid had never seen an Aga cooker before and it took her a week to realise that the rope strung between two apple trees was in fact a washing line and not left over from some children's game, but she soon got into the swing of things and these days when she mentions how nice it would be still to have a flat in London, it's only twice a week rather than twice an hour. I think it's safe to say that we're happy here. We now *own* a house on the Suffolk coast, have an American-sized fridge, big tumble dryer, and a cordless hedge-trimmer, but for me the greatest attraction is being able to have a dip in the North Sea every morning, whatever the weather, whatever the season. Before I get out of bed, Astrid leans over and gives me a sleepy peck on the cheek goodbye.

"In case you don't come back," she says. "I'd feel bad." (BREAKING NEWS! Short Bearded Composer in Orange Trunks Discovered Floating Up Oslofjord Humming *Lovejoy* theme!)

The trick, to year-round outdoor swimming, for the record, is not to miss a day, or you've had it, and not to think too hard about what you're doing, or else you wouldn't do it. In the winter when you first hit the water, the shock of the cold leaves you unable to breathe, various appendages curl, shrivel and disappear, you immediately start to ache, and after about a minute or so it gets so painful you have to get out before you pass out. But other than that it's a fantastic way to start the day, so you may want to try it. It really does get the circulation going.

"Guess that's why you come home blue then," Astrid just said, reading over my shoulder. "The Return of the Popsicle."

My swimming career, and I use the word "swimming"

The bridge to Walberswick beach, en route for my morning swim in the North Sea, January 2003, with Buster the Border Terrier. Photo taken by my wife, still in night attire under her parka, hoping to capture one final image of her loving husband in the event that the undertow carried me halfway to Zeebrugge.

only for convenience, since "immersing myself in water hoping to manage 100 strokes without going under" is a bit of a mouthful – began almost 20 years ago on a sultry July day in London when, to avoid staring at the phone not ringing with lucrative job offers, I wandered over to the Mixed Bathing Pond on Hampstead Heath for an afternoon dip.

It was an extremely pleasurable experience. Far more so than I'd expected – no rusting shopping trolleys snagging my feet, no bicycle tyres floating past, no dead bodies, only the occasional toxic blue algae or irate swan to interfere with my progress to the float and back, and so I went in again the next day, and the next, and the next and then, before I knew it, it was October and the Mixed Pond closed for the season and I was devastated to find the gate locked. A fellow swimmer named Rudolf Strauss, an octogenarian with two knee replacements, informed me that the Men's Pond, across the Heath on the Highgate side, remained open all winter and I should try it. I duly trudged over, thinking if Rudolf can do this, so can I. And I enjoyed myself over there, too. Before you jump to conclusions, allow me to add that the Men's Pond has *no* nude sunbathing at 7am and that we are all *very very butch real he-men* types.

I loved the early morning trek across the Heath with Buster our Border Terrier, I loved the camaraderie among swimmers, the open-air changing rooms, the snow settling on my towel, I even loved the cold-water-only showers which, in fact, felt warm after the pond. Every day Astrid would get the full report: what Terry said to Graham, what Piers said in the *Ham & High,* what Les the lifeguard cooked for breakfast in the lifeguard hut, how many sausages Buster cadged, what the water temperature was, who was home with pneumonia and so on. November turned into December, then January, and the lifeguards kindly chopped a large hole in the ice for us.

"Are you out of your mind?" Astrid said one day when I got home. "I just saw on the news that it's been so cold London Zoo had to bring its penguins indoors." She tells me she used to spend the whole time I was gone, fretting, thinking that any minute the doorbell would go and it'd be the London Ambulance saying there's an ice cube with heart failure across the Heath calling her name and could she come quick. (These days however, I notice she falls peacefully back to sleep, snoring, after my kiss goodbye.)

But I kept at it, and then suddenly it was summer again and I'd managed a whole year! I was proud of myself. I liked the feeling that I was *doing* something, that by 8.30 in the morning at least I'd accomplished *something*, but the driving force these days to get me into the sea is the discipline of it all. It gets me up in the morning. And it makes me feel better. However stressful my night's sleep, however full I might feel from having eaten or drunk too much, however much I sense I'm coming down with a bug, however under par I might feel in general, I know for certain that the swim will improve things. An hour later I might feel like crap again but it's still worth it, trust me.

The North Sea, incidentally, should you ever fancy giving it a go, never gets quite as cold as the Highgate Men's Pond (which is actually the Fleet River), or at least doesn't feel as cold. It does, however, have waves, occasionally a fierce undertow, the odd seal or jellyfish, and there is of course an art to drying off during a Force 10 gale. To assist in this endeavour, and for the purposes of keeping one's balance when getting sand out from between one's toes and or wedding tackle, I highly recommend a type of knapsack which not only converts easily into a canvas stool, but offers convenient buckled compartments for beach shoes, neoprene gloves, hand warmers, dog biscuits, thermometer, plus any compact folding defibrillators one's wife might stick in the bag. My initial swimming group of one has grown to eight over the summer months but falls back down to The Hard Core Four throughout the winter. John, Claire, Jay and DK, plus now latecomers Jan and Viv. None of us wear wetsuits, but swimming gloves, at least for me, are a must. I like my hands fully defrosted when I play the piano.

And play it I do. Often. My treasured 1906 Blüthner grand was given to me by actor Julian Holloway, who'd inherited it from his father, Stanley Holloway, who had acquired it sometime in the 1930s, and it is on this piano that Stanley, who played the original Alfred Doolittle in *My Fair Lady*, learned *Get Me To The Church On Time* and *With A Little Bit Of Luck*. I often used to visit the Holloways out in Buckinghamshire in the Sixties and knew the piano well. After Julian's mother, Laney, passed away, the Blüthner went up for auction along with the rest of Stanley's effects, but when it failed to reach its reserve, Julian, by then in California, rang to say he'd like to give it to me.

I was and still am extremely touched. I went to see the piano where it was stored in Willesden or Acton or somewhere hard to park, to ascertain whether or not it would go up the stairs to my first-floor London studio. I inspected it and happily announced that it would. When it arrived, it didn't even make the first turn and went back to Acton. Eventually, Camden Council stopped traffic, a giant crane made its way up Parliament Hill, a bay window was removed, and the Blüthner was swung into my studio where it remained until it came up here to Suffolk to grace our front hall. I love it. I can hardly walk past without sitting down and playing it.

I play songs, mostly. Classics. Standards. The ones I love. A bit of Gershwin, a bit of Rodgers, Kern, Cole Porter, Irving Berlin, Harold Arlen, Jule Styne, Jimmy Van Heusen – all the greats. I'd play Sondheim if his piano parts weren't so tricky. Only very rarely do I play anything I've written, and then only by request.

"Honey? Play that one you wrote that goes da da-dum, da dada-dum deedlydo."

Celebrating life in Walberswick.

"What?"

"You know. The one I like. With that funny tinkly thing in the middle."

I look at my wife, blankly.

"*You know*," she says, with the same growing impatience I sense when I've forgotten where the Pyrex pie plate goes that I've just dried and she watches me staring helplessly around the kitchen. "That one that reminds me of something else!"

And as I sit there feeling bewildered, I console myself with the fact that even though my brain is clearly not up to that of my wife's, I am an extremely lucky man to be sitting here in Suffolk at all instead of... well. Let me share my recurring nightmare with you.

Years ago, in the old King Brother days, we'd get down to London, late, having done a gig up north, to find the only place open after midnight was the Lotus House Chinese restaurant on the Edgware Road. A guy named Jack, probably in his 50s but to me looking at least 100, would be playing the piano while uninterested diners wolfed down their sweet and sour pork. Nobody took much notice of him apart from me. I was fascinated because for some reason he always added an extra beat after the first line of *Isn't It Romantic?* and it became a moment I rather looked forward to. He never once got it right.

Every so often I wake up in the wee small hours, sweating, thinking I'm him, and that after my long and varied career, after all I've managed to accomplish, there I am, ending my days playing *Isn't It Romantic?* at the Lotus House, Edgware Road... badly.

But then I remember that I'm actually here in Suffolk with Astrid asleep by my side, the East Anglian waves crashing in the distance, and that beautiful piano downstairs waiting patiently for my attention.

Now. Isn't *that* romantic?

My 60th birthday bash at Robert and Babs Powell's. Astrid seems to have her eyes on the food. At least that's what she told me.

Three Kings wearing sunglasses in the land of the midnight sun. Drøbak, Norway, 2013.

Three King Brothers and a sister. Michael, me, Tony (seated), and Moira. Suffolk, 2012.

Enjoying a slice of the Algarve, 1994.

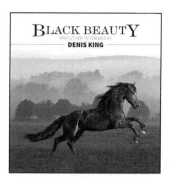

**A new compilation available
to download from Amazon, iTunes,
and other online retailers**

*Denis got his break in television by writing the theme
for* The Adventures of Black Beauty – *which not only
won him an Ivor Novello Award but went on to be voted
Britain's second-most popular TV theme of all time.
Denis has composed the music for more than 200
television series, including* Lovejoy, *and has chosen 14
of his favourites for this new album.*

Black Beauty (Galloping Home)
Ivor Novello Award-winning theme for the popular
London Weekend Television series.

We'll Meet Again
Drama series starring Susannah York set in and around
US Air Force bases in East Anglia during World War II.

Dick Turpin
Adventure series based on the notorious highwayman,
starring Richard O'Sullivan.

All At Number 20
Thames TV sitcom starring Maureen Lipman

Within These Walls
Drama series set in a women's prison, starring Googie Withers

Taking The Floor
BBC comedy series about a young couple obsessed with Latin American ballroom dancing.

Wish Me Luck
London Weekend TV wartime drama series set in occupied France.

Lovejoy
BBC comedy-drama series, starring Ian McShane as a lovable rogue antiques dealer.

About Face
Central TV series starring Maureen Lipman playing different characters each week.

A Day To Remember
Written by Jack Rosenthal, a tragi-comedy about memory loss, starring George Cole.

Hannay
Thames TV drama series based on John Buchan's famous character, starring Robert Powell.

Moon & Son
BBC 13-part comedy thriller set in England and France starring Millicent Martin as a clairvoyant.

Running Wild
London Weekend sitcom starring Ray Brooks as an irresponsible gambler.

Between The Wars
Set between 1918 and 1939, a London Weekend drama series based on various authors' novels of the period.

Printed in Germany
by Amazon Distribution
GmbH, Leipzig